100
TECHNIQUES
for
PROFESSIONAL WEDDING PHOTOGRAPHERS

BILL HURTER

AMHERST MEDIA, INC. ■ BUFFALO, NY

ABOUT THE AUTHOR

Bill Hurter has been involved in the photographic industry for the past thirty years. He is the former editor of *Petersen's PhotoGraphic* magazine and currently the editor of both *AfterCapture* and *Rangefinder* magazines. He has authored over thirty books on photography and hundreds of articles on photography and photographic technique. He is a graduate of American University and Brooks Institute of Photography, from which he holds a BFA and Honorary Masters of Science and Masters of Fine Art degrees. He is currently a member of the Brooks Board of Governors. Early in his career, he covered Capital Hill during the Watergate Hearings and worked for three seasons as a stringer for the L.A. Dodgers. He is married and lives in West Covina, CA.

Front cover photograph by Tom Muñoz.
Back cover photograph by Bruce Dorn.

Published by:
Amherst Media, Inc.
P.O. Box 586
Buffalo, N.Y. 14226
Fax: 716-874-4508
www.AmherstMedia.com

Publisher: Craig Alesse
Senior Editor/Production Manager: Michelle Perkins
Assistant Editor: Barbara A. Lynch-Johnt
Editorial Assistance from: John S. Loder, Carey A. Maines, Charles Schweizer

ISBN-13: 978-1-58428-245-7
Library of Congress Control Number: 2007926665
Printed in Korea.
10 9 8 7 6 5 4 3 2 1

TABLE OF CONTENTS

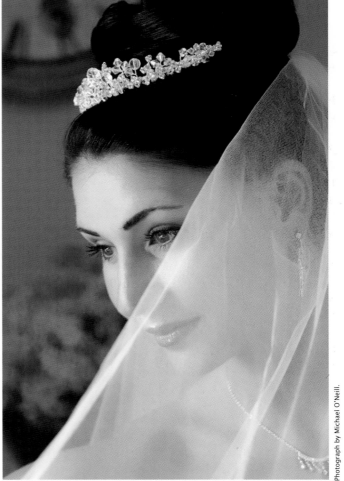

Photograph by Michael O'Neill.

Photograph by Bruce Dorn.

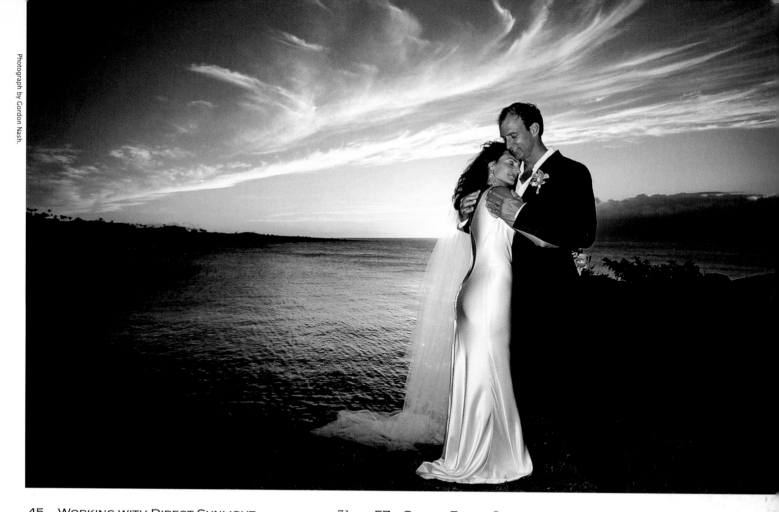

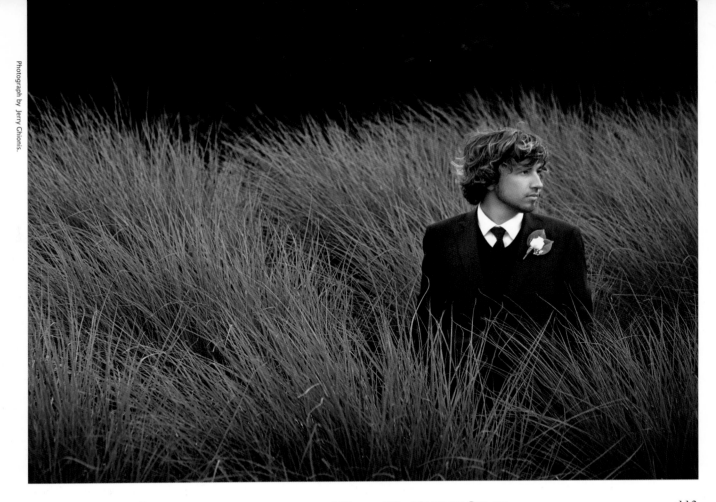

Photograph by Jerry Ghionis.

WHAT MAKES A GREAT WEDDING PHOTOGRAPHER?

A sense of fashion and style is all-important to the wedding captures. Nick Adams created a bold cropping in order to isolate the beautiful features and necklaces of this bride. Nick used a 4x3-foot softbox as a main light and two monolights behind a 6x8-foot scrim. The two main light sources were used on either side of the camera. The fill lights were dialed way down in intensity for this shot. Reflectors were used at either side of the model to help redirect stray light. A monolight with beauty dish was also used and placed about nine feet high and angled down to create an elegant hair light.

The rewards of being a successful professional wedding photographer are great—not only financially, but also in terms of community status. The wedding photographer of the new millennium is not regarded merely as a craftsman, but as an artist and an important member of the community.

Through my association with Wedding and Portrait Photographers International (WPPI) and *Rangefinder* magazine, I talk to hundreds of wedding photographers each year. So, in preparing the text for this book, I drew on our conversations as I searched for the right words to define what makes "great" wedding photography and, consequently, "great" wedding photographers. The following are a few qualities they seem to share.

Consistency. Consistency is surely one ingredient of greatness. Those photographers who produce splendid albums each time out are well on their way to greatness.

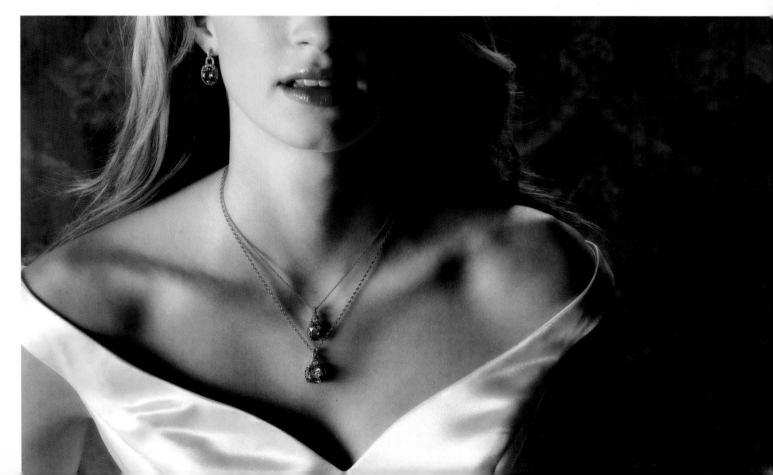

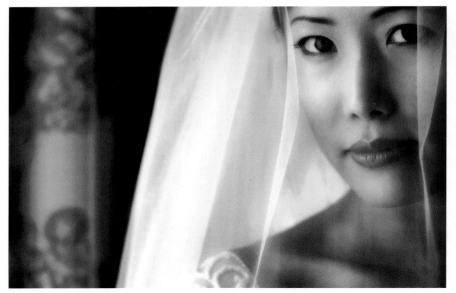

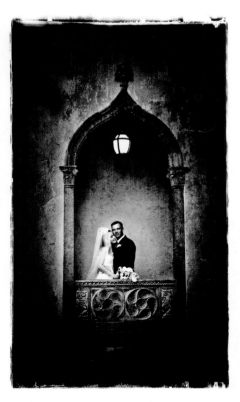

LEFT—Charles Maring blends fashion and editorial coverage into all his wedding shots. Here, a shot of the bride through the veil is executed as if it were a spread to the opening of an article, with negative space to the left and tight cropping on the bride's face. **RIGHT**—Some wedding photographers take style to the next level. Michael Schuhmann, for example, says of his work, "It's different; it's fashion, it's style." This image is quite unlike the original capture, having been altered considerably in Photoshop.

Likability. A common thread among the really good ones is affability and likability. They are fully at ease with other people and they have a sense of personal confidence that inspires trust. For example, acclaimed photographer David Williams says, "I just love it when people think I'm a friend of the couple—someone they just haven't met yet who happens to do photography." Maximizing these personal interactions allows the best wedding photographers to create animated, filled-with-life portraits—images that bring out of the real personality and vitality of the subject.

Cool Under Pressure. The ability to work under pressure is also critical. To be successful, wedding photographers must not only master a variety of types of photography but also perform them in a very limited time frame. The couple and their families have made months of detailed preparations (not to mention a considerable financial investment) for this once-in-a-lifetime event, and expectations are high. Couples don't just want a photographic "record" of the day's events, they want inspired, imaginative images and an unforgettable presentation—and there are no second chances. This means that, aside from technical skills, achieving success requires calm nerves and the ability to perform at the highest levels under stress. This pressure is why many gifted photographers do not pursue wedding photography as their main occupation.

Up to Date. To stay on the cutting edge, the leading wedding photographers also scour bridal magazines, studying the latest looks in editorial and advertising photography. These magazines are what prospective

SUCCESS REQUIRES
CALM NERVES AND THE ABILITY
TO PERFORM AT THE HIGHEST
LEVELS UNDER STRESS.

brides look at and want to see in their own wedding images. Consequently, editorial style has become a huge influence on wedding photography—perhaps the single biggest influence at this writing. Noted Australian wedding photographer Martin Schembri calls the style of the contemporary wedding coverage a "magazine" style with a "clean, straight look."

A Great Observer. The truly gifted wedding photographer is also a great observer. He or she sees and captures the myriad of special, fleeting moments that often go unrecorded. Through keen observation, a skill set that can be clearly enhanced through practice, the photographer begins to

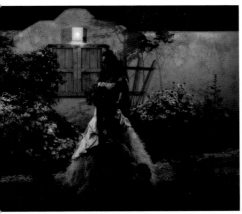

Nick Adams does remarkable bridal formals. Of this image he says, "This session started a couple of hours earlier, but we found ourselves working well after sundown, so I had to light everything that I wanted to see in the photograph. I used one monolight shooting into a 4-foot umbrella for a main light, powered by a portable battery. It was set about seven or eight feet high and feathered a little in front of the subject. Two Nikon SB800s added light to the back part of the scene, one on each side. I needed these lights to do three things: 1) light the wall, 2) light the garden flowers and ground behind the bride, and 3) add some edge light to the bride. I put the plastic diffuser caps on them to make the light less directional and raised them up about nine or ten feet high, angled about 45 degrees down to light the faces of the flowers—sort of like sunlight." Nick has gotten pretty good at this type of on-location problem solving, adding, "I check my lighting while I work, using test images. With the histogram and image review (and a lot of practice!) I can work quickly on location without a light meter." The second shot included here shows the effect of the background lights without the umbrella main light.

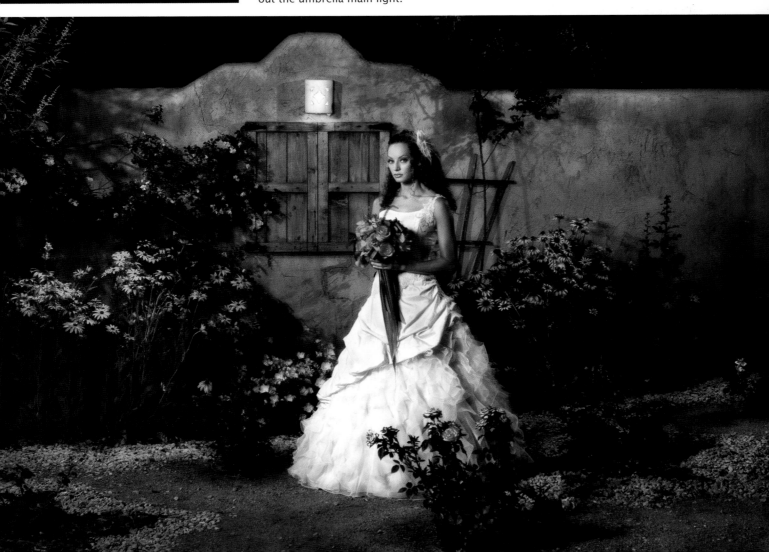

develop the knack of predicting what will happen next and making sure he or she is ready to capture it. The more weddings you photograph, the more accustomed you become to their rhythm and flow—but the sense of anticipation is also a function of clearly seeing what is transpiring in front of you and reacting to it quickly.

The Ability to Idealize. Another trait that separates the competent photographer from the great one is the ability to idealize. The exceptional photographer produces images in which the people look great. This means that the photographer must be skilled at hiding pounds and recognizing a person's "best side." This recognition must be instantaneous and the pho-

ANOTHER TRAIT THAT SEPARATES THE COMPETENT PHOTOGRAPHER FROM THE GREAT ONE IS THE ABILITY TO IDEALIZE.

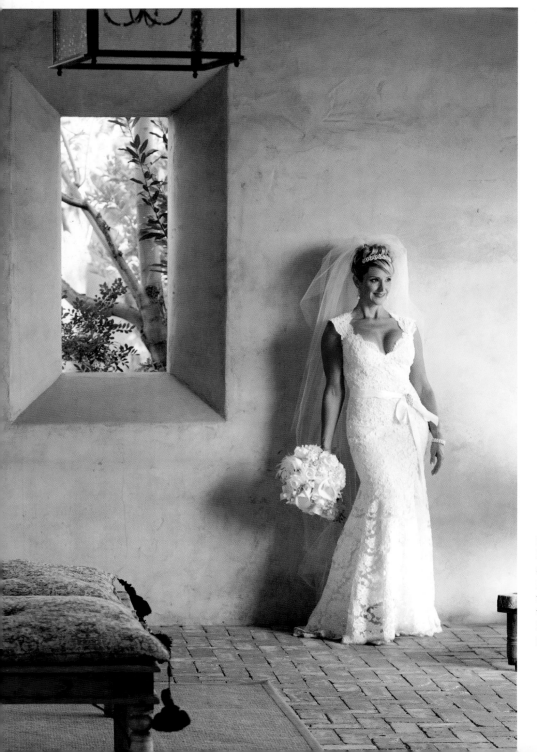

Ken Sklute is a master at idealizing his brides. Here, she appears to be leaning against the adobe wall—but she actually isn't; this would cause her to look larger to the camera. Ken used the beautiful portico lighting and a wonderful pose, looking away from the camera, to bring out the innate beauty of this lovely bride.

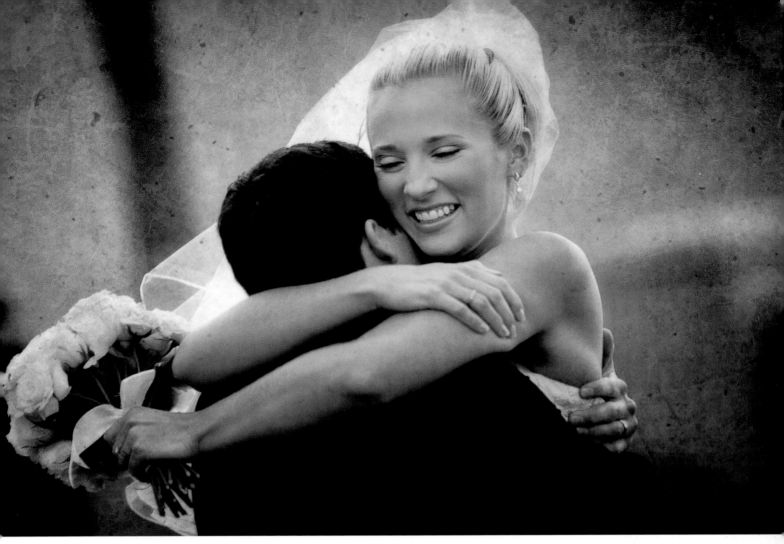

Michael Schuhmann has a great sense of timing. Here, he captured the unbridled joy of the bride in a loving embrace. Timing like this is honed over time and nurtured with careful observation. The background of the image is a textured layer created in Photoshop. You can see that the layer does not appear in the bride's skin, only in the background.

tographer must have the skills to quickly and fluidly make any needed adjustments in the pictures. Through careful choice of camera angles, poses, and lighting, many of these "imperfections" can be made unnoticeable. This is especially important when it comes to the bride, who must be made to look as beautiful as possible. Most women spend more time and money on their appearance for their wedding day than for any other day in their lives, and photographs should chronicle that.

Creative Vision. David Anthony Williams, an inspired Australian wedding and portrait photographer, believes that the key ingredient to great wedding photos is something he once read that was attributed to the great Magnum photographer Elliot Erwitt: "Good photography is not about zone printing or any other Ansel-Adams nonsense. It's about seeing. You either see or you don't see. The rest is academic. Photography is simply a function of noticing things. Nothing more."

Williams adds to this, "Good wedding photography is not about complicated posing, painted backdrops, sumptuous backgrounds, or five lights used brilliantly. It is about expression, interaction, and life! The rest is important, but secondary."

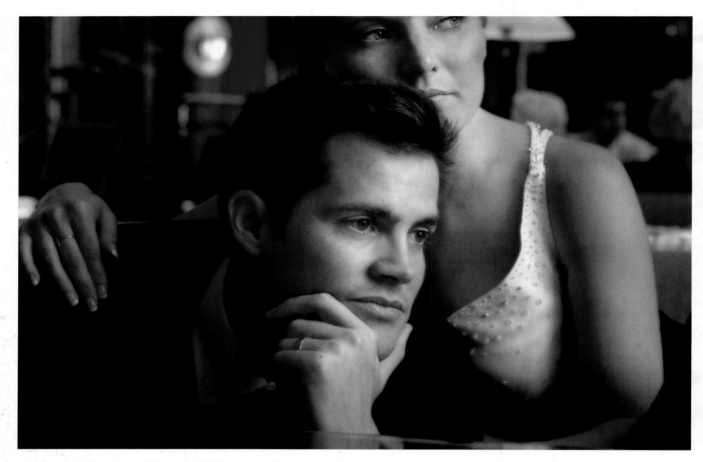

Immersion. In talking to Williams, and a great many other very successful wedding photographers, another common factor in achieving success (and an experience they all talk about) is total immersion. They involve themselves in the event and with the people. Celebrated wedding photographer Joe Buissink has described this as "being in the moment," a Zen-like state that at least for him is physically and emotionally exhausting. Buissink stays in the moment from the time he begins shooting and will stay in that mode for six to eight hours. It's interaction and communication, but also a little magic. (At the same time, of course, you cannot be drawn into the events to the extent that you lose your sense of objectivity or stop paying attention to what's going on around you.)

Even when a wedding image is posed, David Williams seems to melt into the background, allowing his couple to dictate the emotional content of the image. As Williams says, great wedding photography is not about technique, it's about "expression, interaction, and life."

100
TECHNIQUES

1. DEVELOP YOUR PEOPLE SKILLS

To be a successful wedding photographer you have to be a "people person," someone who is capable of inspiring trust in the bride and groom. Interaction with the participants at crucial and often very stressful moments during the wedding day is inevitable, and that is when the photographer with people skills really shines.

Elite wedding photographer Joe Buissink, for example, has been labeled a "salt of the earth" personality who makes his clients instantly like and trust him. That trust leads to complete freedom to capture the event as he sees it. It also helps that Buissink sees each wedding ceremony as significant and treats the day with great respect. Buissink advises, "You must hone your communication skills to create a personal rapport with clients, so they will invite you to participate in their special moments." And he stresses the im-

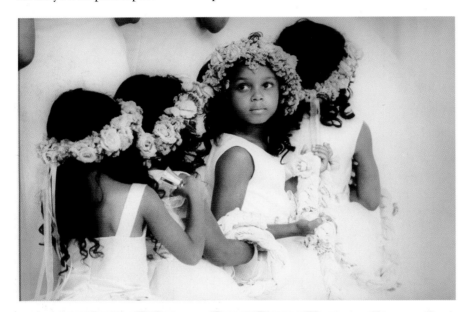

Joe Buissink is not only the observer, he is the cinematographer, capable of framing an event simultaneously with its occurrence.

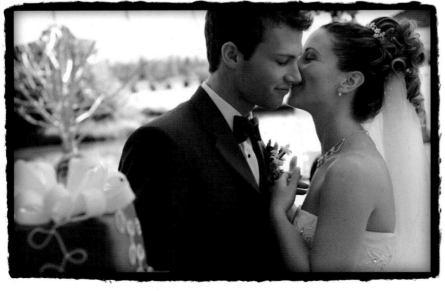

Kevin Kubota encourages his brides and grooms to "wear their emotions on their sleeves," which produces wonderful images like this.

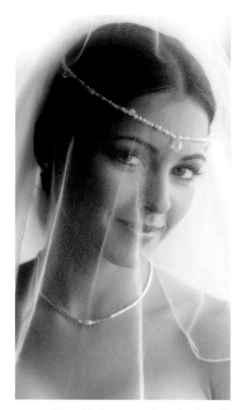

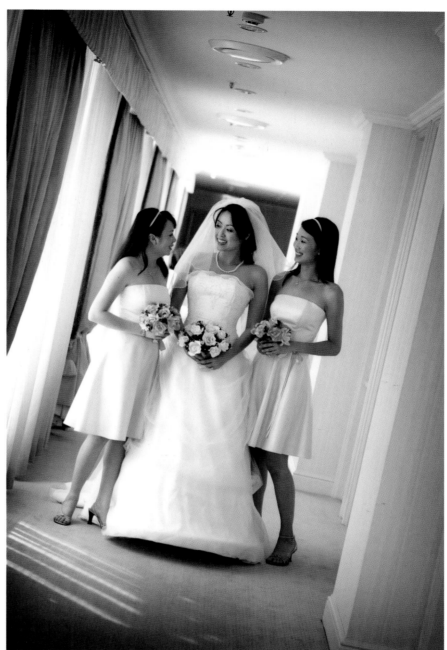

ABOVE—Tom Muñoz says that simply telling a bride how beautiful she looks can change how she photographs and how she perceives being photographed. There is no doubt that Tom captured the beauty of this bride. **RIGHT**—Posed or natural? Who can be sure? What is evident is Marcus Bell's exquisite sense of timing in capturing the subtle gesture.

portance of being objective and unencumbered. "Leave your personal baggage at home," he says, "this will allow you to balance the three principle roles of observer, director, and psychologist."

Kevin Kubota, a successful wedding and portrait photographer from the Pacific Northwest, always encourages his couples to be themselves and to wear their emotions on their sleeves—an instruction that resonates throughout the entire day. He also tries to get to know them as much as possible before the wedding and encourages his brides and grooms to share their own ideas. This establishes a feeling of mutual trust between client and photographer.

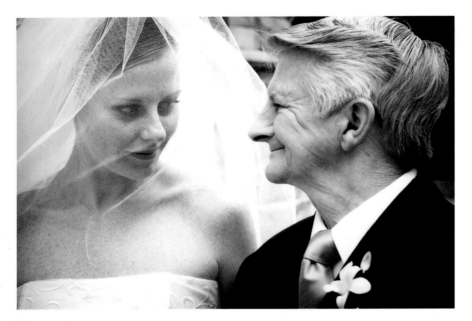

Master wedding photographer Tom Muñoz notes that a little flattery goes a long way. "When we're photographing the bride, we treat her like she's a princess," Muñoz says. "Besides knowing how to pose a woman, one of the biggest things that changes her posture and expression is what you tell her. We're not dealing with models—and as stupid as it sounds, telling a bride how beautiful she looks changes how she photographs and how she perceives being photographed. It becomes a positive experience rather than a time-consuming, annoying one. The same thing goes for the groom," Tom states. "His chest pumps up, he arches his back; they fall right into it. It's very cute."

2. RECOGNIZE WHAT'S SPECIAL

Greg Gibson, a two-time Pulitzer-Prize winning journalist turned wedding photographer says, "All weddings are alike on some level—there's a couple in love, they're going to have this big party, there's the anticipation, the preparation, the ceremony, the party. It's like the movie *Groundhog Day*. The challenge is to find the nuances in each event." Every wedding offers new experiences and new challenges, and this is what Gibson says keeps him fresh through fifty weddings per year. "It's fun. When I go to a wedding, people are always glad to see me, I'm welcomed in. When I was a journalist that wasn't always the case; Monica [Lewinsky] wasn't happy to see me when I showed up at the Mayflower Hotel." This allows him to remain unobtrusive and not impose on moments that should remain natural and genuine, a primary means of preserving a wedding's uniqueness.

Perhaps because of its romantic nature, photographers who are also born romantics often find it easier to capture the special relationship shared by each couple. As photographer Michael Schuhmann says, "I love to pho-

BORN ROMANTICS OFTEN FIND IT EASIER TO CAPTURE THE SPECIAL RELATIONSHIP SHARED BY EACH COUPLE.

THE UNIQUENESS OF THE EVENT
WILL ALSO REVEAL ITSELF
MORE FULLY WHEN THE DAY
IS VIEWED AS A STORY.

tograph people who are in love and are comfortable expressing it—if they are so in love that they can't contain it, then it's real." Being a romantic is not completely necessary, of course—after all, weddings are celebrations, which means they are also about having fun. The wedding photographer gets to be part of this joy.

The uniqueness of the event will also reveal itself more fully when the day is viewed as a story. By linking the spontaneous events of the day, sensitive portrayals that highlight the emotions elicited, you can build a visual narrative that sets each wedding apart from all others. This what the modern bride wants to see in her wedding coverage.

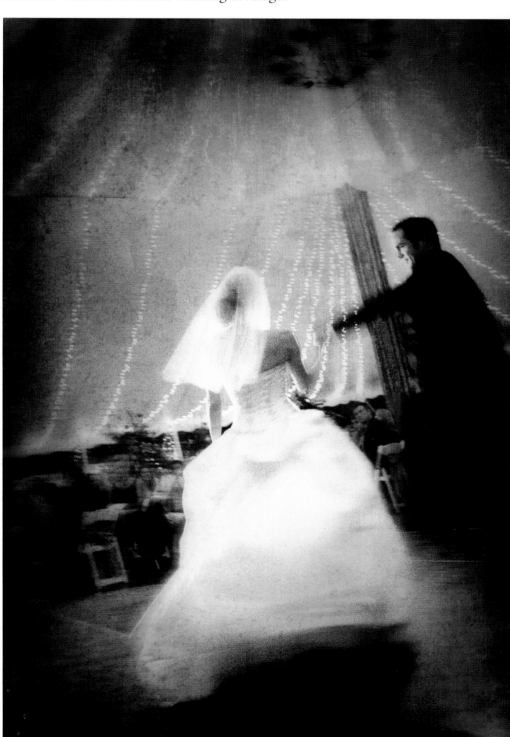

Michael Schuhmann says, "I love to photograph people who are in love and are comfortable expressing it or are so in love that they can't contain it, then it's real."

CAPTURE ALL THE DETAILS

According to wedding specialist Michael O'Neill, "When I first started photographing weddings (in the last millennium) the owner of the studio I worked for would have your head if you shot more than 120 exposures on even the most extravagant wedding. Today, I routinely shoot ten times that amount." Many of

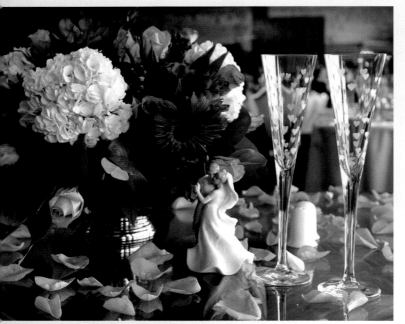

these shots show the details of the day. "Today's brides and grooms expect to see *all* of their wedding day," adds Michael. "Shoot details. Shoot closeups. Flowers, rings, dress details, jewelry, shoes, architecture, landscapes, table settings, menus, champagne glasses, cake decorations, etc. The detail shots are almost as important to today's client as the portraits." Details aren't always *things*, of course, Michael notes. "Shoot candid shots all day long. Take shots of the bridesmaids helping the bride get dressed and the flower girl's antics during the ceremony. And don't limit yourself to action shots—get reaction shots. When the couple exchanges vows, whirl around and capture the look on their parents' faces. Great storytelling includes both actions and reactions."

LEFT—Here is a detail shot of the couple's champagne glasses and cake-top decoration. This was principally an available-light exposure created using the natural light streaming in through a window to the right of the table. The light was supplemented by bounce light off the ceiling from a camera-mounted Nikon SB-800 speedlight set on TTL (at –1EV). Photograph by Michael O'Neill. **BELOW**—Here, the bride posed on the floor by a fireplace. The main light was an off-camera, radio-fired Vivitar 285 HV flash. The fill light was provided by a camera-mounted Nikon SB-800 set in automatic mode (at –2EV). The camera was in manual exposure mode. The image was converted to sepia and selectively colored in Photoshop. Photograph by Michael O'Neill.

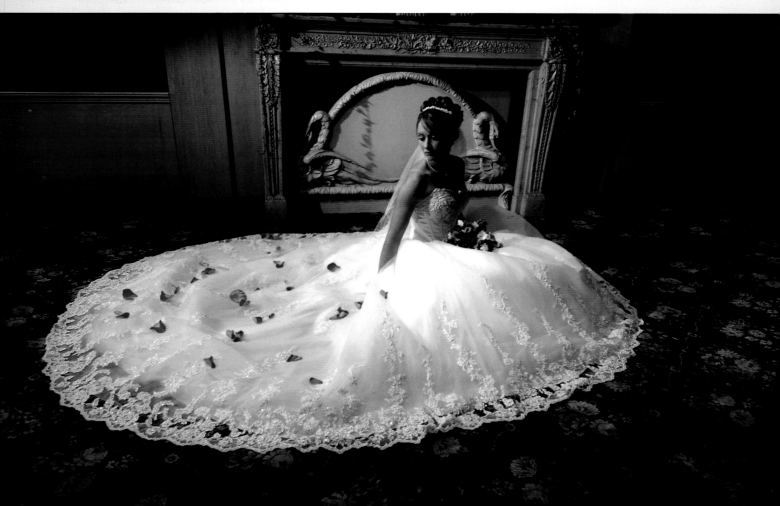

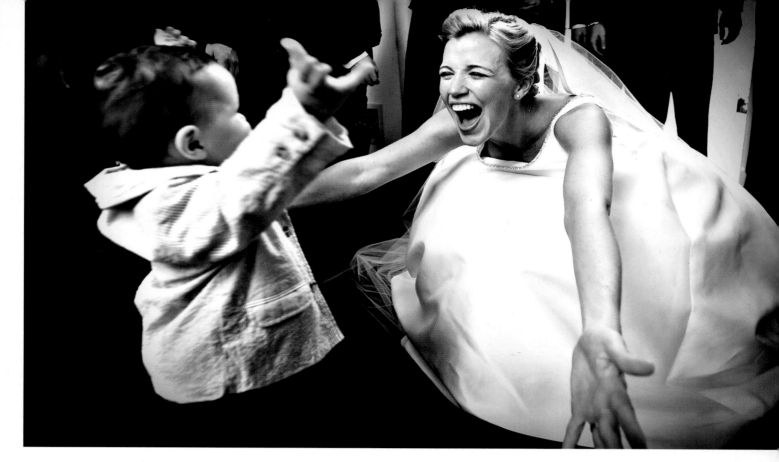

No one has better reactions and storytelling skills than a Pulitzer Prize-winning photojournalist. Here, Greg Gibson captured the full gamut of emotion as these two connected.

3. SHOOT PEAK ACTION

Sports photographers learn to react to an event by anticipating where and when the exposure must be made. A pole-vaulter, for example, is ascending at one moment and falling the next—and right in between there is an instant of peak action that the photographer strives to isolate. Even with high burst rates, however, it is not a question of blanketing a scene with high-speed exposures; it is knowing when to press the shutter release. With a good sense of timing and solid observation skills, you will drastically increase your chances for successful exposures in wedding situations. By being prepared for each event, being ever alert, and refining your reaction time you can also improve your odds.

Be Prepared. Being prepared to capture each moment starts with doing your homework. The more you know about the scheduled events and their order, the better you can prepare to cover those events as effectively as possible. Discussing the wedding plans with the other vendors involved (the wedding planner, DJ, caterer, officiant, etc.) and visiting each venue is an excellent way to prepare (see page 86). What you learn is critical to developing your game plan; it will allow you to choreograph your movements so that you are in the optimum position for each phase of the wedding day. The confidence that this kind of preparation provides is also immeasurable.

Observe and React Quickly. Within this framework of "planned" events, however, you should always be watching and monitoring each mo-

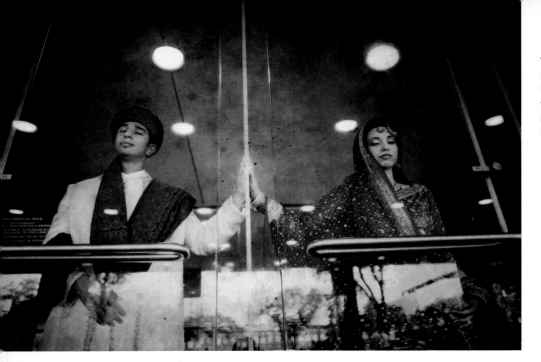

This is one of my favorite wedding images by Jesh de Rox. It depicts the serenity and bliss of the couple, yet we are prevented from entering their sphere by plate glass. It is a uniquely spiritual moment captured by expecting the unexpected.

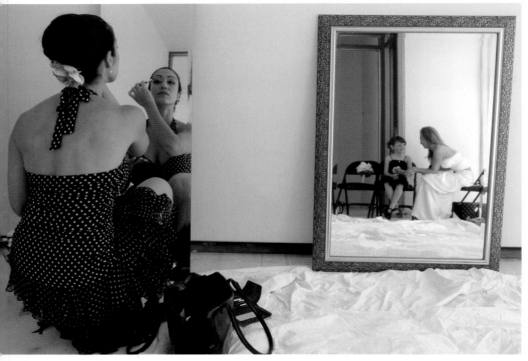

Timing is everything. This is a Joe Buissink shot, which he may or may not have choreographed. What is evident is that he captured both scenes at the peak of interest simultaneously. That's good reflexes.

ment as it unfolds around you—and this usually means watching more than one event at a time. Keep your camera constantly at the ready. You may want to leave it in one of the AE modes so there are no exposure adjustments to be made. Simply raise the camera, compose, and shoot.

With quiet observation, many wonderful moments can be captured. Being able to do this effectively is a function of completely trusting yourself to translate input into instant reaction. Master wedding photojournalist Joe Buissink says, "Trust your intuition. Do not think. Just react or it will be too late."

4. WORK UNOBTRUSIVELY

Traditional wedding coverage would feature dozens of posed pictures pulled from a shot list that was often passed down by generations of other traditional wedding photographers. There may have been as many as seventy-five scripted shots—from cutting the cake, to tossing the garter, to the father of the bride walking his daughter down the aisle. In addition to the scripted moments, traditional photographers filled in the album with "candids," many of which were staged (or at least made with the subjects aware of the camera).

YOU SHOULD BE LISTENING AND WATCHING, SENSITIVE TO WHAT IS HAPPENING AND READY TO REACT.

The contemporary wedding photographer's approach is quite different. Instead of being a part of every event, moving people around and staging the action, the photographer tends to be quietly invisible, fading into the background so the subjects are not aware of the photographer's presence. Rather than intruding on the scene, the photographer documents it from a distance—usually with longer lenses and natural light. When people are not aware they are being photographed, they are more likely to act like themselves. Moving quietly through the event, you should be listening and watching, sensitive to what is happening and ready to react.

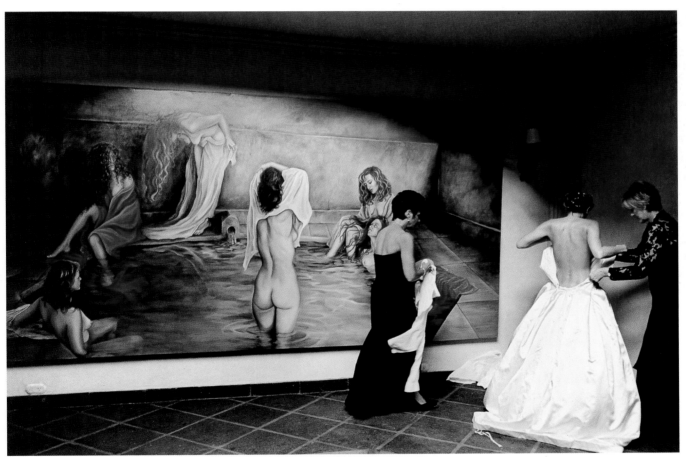

There is no shot-list entry for this image by Joe Buissink, who shoots most of his weddings on film. Joe is a keen observer and knows a great shot in the making when he sees one.

Of course, flying under the radar doesn't have to mean remaining totally aloof. Describing his brand of wedding photojournalism, Greg Gibson says, "I'm not a true fly on the wall. I interact with the client. There are two camps of photojournalists. There are the ones who want to be totally invisible, the one who won't talk or interact. I'm definitely in the other camp. I laugh and joke with the client, get them to relax with my presence. We're

IS IT POSING OR DIRECTING?

When Marcus Bell creates a bridal portrait, he begins by observing the bride, making mental notes of what he'd like to see. Then, if he can't replicate the nuance, he'll ask the bride to do what he saw. For instance, he once saw a bride walking with her head down, then look up and smile at just the right moment. Marcus tried having her replicate the walk a few times, hoping to capture a similar spontaneous moment, but she didn't look up. So he simply asked her to look up while she was walking. This kept the flow going while allowing him to capture a nuanced and genuine moment.

Greg Gibson, an award-winning photojournalist turned wedding photographer, has a similar unobtrusive approach. As he says, "My clients are professional people. They want to enjoy their day and not be encumbered by posing for pictures. So I try to take advantage of the resources at a wedding. If a bride is getting dressed in an area with bad light I may say, 'Can we come over here and do this?' I don't try to create moments, though, or impose something on their day by saying, 'Let me get you and your mother hugging.' I try to let those things happen spontaneously and use my background and experience to put myself in the right position to anticipate those moments."

As if invisible, Greg Gibson captures a splendid moment on the wedding day. A slightly longer than normal lens removed him physically from the scene. The rest is just timing and intuition.

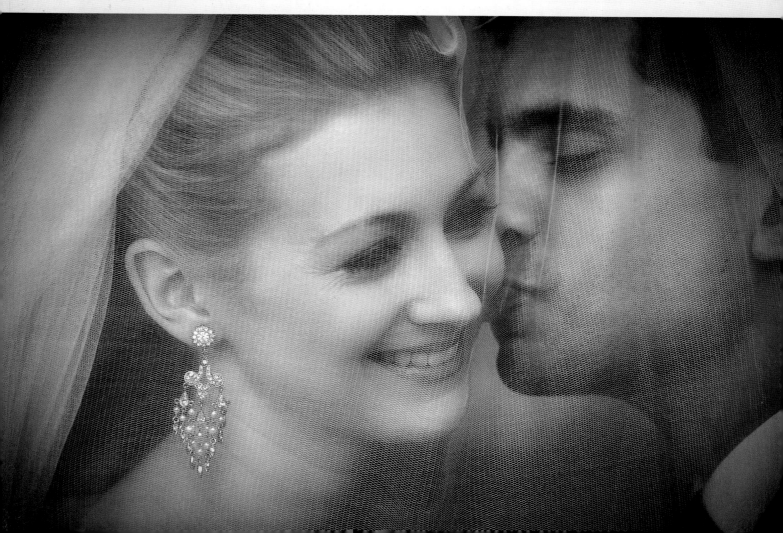

going to spend a lot of time together and I don't want them to feel like there's a stranger in the room. If I find myself constantly in conversations with the bride and family members, then I withdraw a bit. I don't want to be talking and not taking photos."

5. SYNC YOUR CAMERAS

Wedding photographer Chris Becker offers this tip: if shooting with multiple camera bodies, be sure to synchronize the internal clocks on the cameras. This will make it much easier to sequentially organize your images.

6. PACK THREE CAMERA BAGS: A TIP FROM MARCUS BELL

As the saying goes, "Luck favors the prepared." That's Marcus Bell's approach to packing his gear for a wedding. He uses three small bags. Here's what he places in each:

Main Bag
- Spare batteries
- Breath freshener ("A courtesy," he says.)
- Air brush and lens-cleaning cloth
- Two Canon EOS 5Ds
- Two main lenses: 28–70mm f/2.8 and 85mm f/1.2
- 70–200mm f/2.8 lens for ceremony
- Epson P4000 downloader (carried in pocket)
- Point-and-shoot 8MP camera for backup (surprisingly, some of the album images get made with this camera)
- Digital flashmeter
- Flashlight for looking through the three bags
- Stain Stick and spare cloth (to get any stain out of the wedding dress)

Waist Bag (Worn All Day)
- Secondary lenses (35mm f/1.4 and 17–35mm f/2.8)
- Crochet hook (sometimes need to help fasten the bride's dress)
- Arctic Butterfly (a battery-powered sensor-cleaning brush)
- Small handheld video light (battery powered)
- Extension tube for closeups
- More spare batteries
- 30GB worth of CF cards, 4GB capacity each

Backup Bag
- EOS 1D Mark II
- 85mm f/1.8 and 50mm f/1.4 lenses

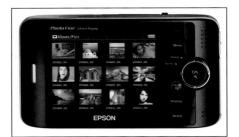

Featuring a high-capacity 80GB hard drive and 3.8-inch LCD, the EPSON P4000 enables users to view, store, and play back photos, videos, and music—all without a computer. This compact battery-operated hard drive/viewer is ideal for downloading and previewing images on site. It is also an excellent way to clear memory cards for continued use.

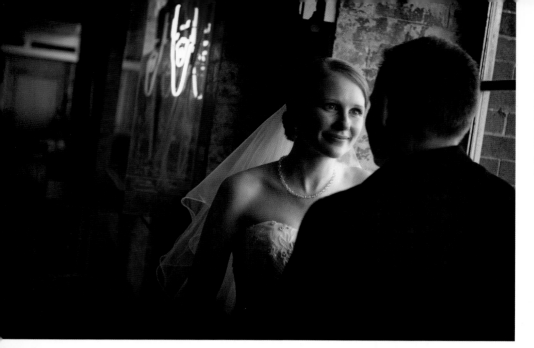

Marcus Bell is prepared for any contingency. In the top image, a wonderful portrait of the bride and groom emerges from a dimly lit pub. In the bottom image, a brightly backlit scene formed beautiful geometric circles on the veil. On-camera flash brought out all of the details in the scene. Preparation is one of the keys to success as a wedding photographer.

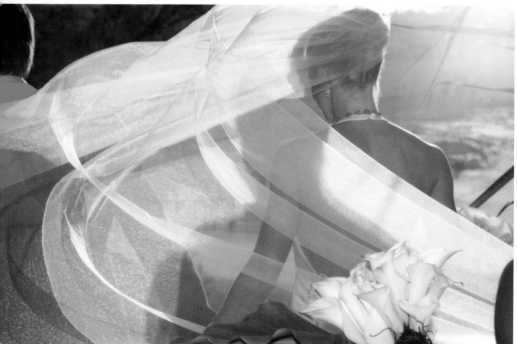

- Tele-extender (rarely used, but kept in the backup bag nonetheless)
- More spare batteries
- Charger for batteries
- Timetable sheet for events and instructions on how to get there

7. HAVE BACKUP AND EMERGENCY EQUIPMENT

Wedding photographers live by Murphy's Law: if anything can go wrong, it will go wrong. That is why most seasoned pros carry backups—extra camera bodies, flash heads, transmitters, batteries, cords, twice the required amount of film or storage cards, etc. For AC-powered flash, extra extension cords, several rolls of duct tape (for taping cords to the floor), power strips, flash tubes, and modeling lights also need to be on hand. Other items of note include a stepladder for making groups shots, flashlights, a mini tool kit (for mini emergencies), and quick-release plates for your tripods (these always seem to get left behind on a table or left attached to a camera).

Spare batteries are also a must. Today's camera batteries are much better than in years past and should last all day without replacement. However, it's always a good idea to bring extra batteries and a charger or two. Spare packs should be fully charged and ready to go—and you should have enough to handle your cameras as well as your assistant's cameras and the backup gear. If downloading images to a laptop, do not forget spare laptop batteries or the computer's AC adapter.

8. Clean Your Image Sensor

The image sensor in a digital camera must be kept clean in order to perform to its optimum level—otherwise, spots may appear on your images. Canon digital cameras have a built-in sensor-cleaning mode. This lifts the camera's reflex mirror so that light air from an air syringe can be used to gently remove any foreign matter. Turning the camera off resets the mirror. The newest DSLRs feature a sonic vibration sensor-cleaning mode that is fully automatic and does not involve you having to touch the sensor all. (*Note:* The image sensor is an extremely delicate device. Do not use compressed air cans to clean it; these have airborne propellants that can coat the sensor in a fine mist, worsening the situation.)

THE IMAGE SENSOR IN A DIGITAL CAMERA MUST BE KEPT CLEAN IN ORDER TO PERFORM TO ITS OPTIMUM LEVEL.

One of the prerequisites of good group photography at weddings is that all of the group members look good, as in this priceless shot of six fairy flowergirls. Photograph by Jessica Claire.

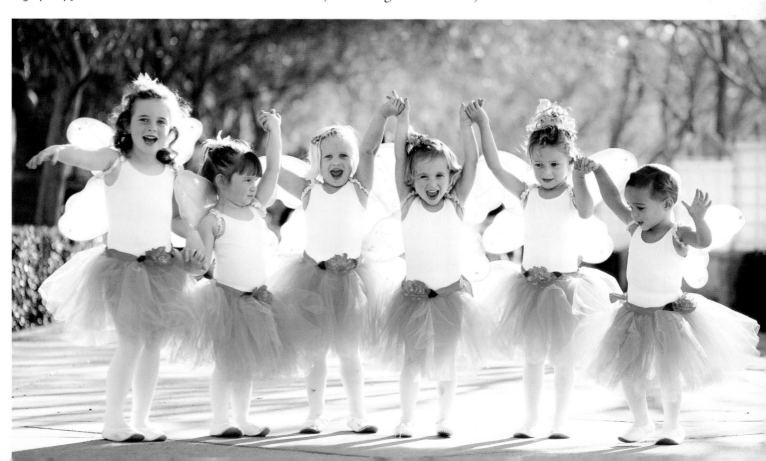

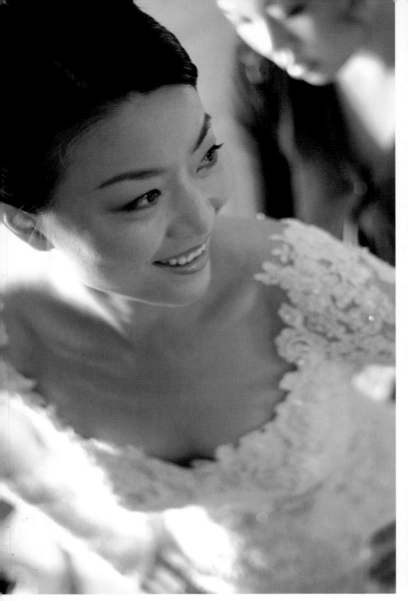

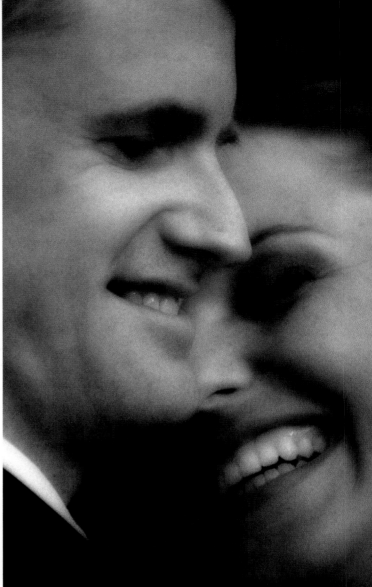

9. MAKE CALCULATED LENS CHOICES

When selecting lenses for wedding photography, speed must be a primary concern. Fast lenses (f/2.8, f/2, f/1.8, f/1.4, f/1.2, etc.) afford many more available-light opportunities than slower speed lenses—a valuable asset when shooting in churches, dim reception venues, and in other low-light conditions. Marcus Bell calls his Canon 35mm f/1.4L USM lens his favorite. Working at dusk with a high ISO setting, he can shoot wide open and mix lighting sources for unparalleled results.

Prime or Zoom? Another concern is whether to use prime (fixed focal-length) lenses or zoom lenses. Faster prime lenses will get lots of use, as they afford many more "available light" opportunities than slower speed lenses. Although modern zoom lenses, particularly those designed for digital SLRs, are extremely sharp, many photographers insist that a multipurpose lens cannot possibly be as sharp as a prime lens, which is optimized for use at a single focal length. Mike Colón, a talented photographer from the

LEFT—Mike Colón prefers prime lenses. One of the best-kept secrets is the standard lens, in this case a 50mm f/1.4, which becomes a 75mm f/1.4 on the Nikon D2X. This image, shot wide open, reveals a shallow depth of field and high image sharpness and contrast. **RIGHT**—One of the reasons the 80–200mm and 70–200mm lenses are so popular is the wide range of framing and cropping possibilities they offer. Here, David Beckstead used a Nikon 80–200mm f/2.8D ED lens at the 175mm setting to get this marvelous closeup of the bride and groom.

San Diego area, uses prime lenses (not zooms) in his wedding coverage and shoots at wide-open apertures most of the time to minimize background distractions. He says, "The telephoto lens is my first choice, because it allows me to be far enough away to avoid drawing attention to myself but close enough to clearly capture the moment. Wide-angle lenses, however, are great for shooting from the hip. I can grab unexpected moments all around me without even looking through the lens."

Zoom lenses are also extremely popular however, and offer unbeatable versatility, allowing you to move quickly from wide to tight views. A common choice seems to be the 80–200mm f/2.8 (Nikon) or the 70–200mm f/2.8 (Canon and Nikon). These are very fast, lightweight lenses that offer a wide variety of useful focal lengths for both the ceremony and reception. They are internal focusing, meaning that the autofocus is lightning fast and the lens does not change length as it is zoomed or focused. At the shortest range, either of these lenses is perfect for creating full- and three-quarter-length portraits. At the long end, the 200mm setting is ideal for tightly cropped, candid shots or head-and-shoulders portraits. These zoom lenses also feature fixed maximum apertures, which do not change as the lens is zoomed. This is a prerequisite for any lens to be used in fast-changing conditions. Lenses with variable maximum apertures provide a cost savings but are not as functional nor as bright in the viewfinder as the faster, fixed-aperture lenses.

ZOOM LENSES . . . OFFER UNBEATABLE VERSATILITY, ALLOWING YOU TO MOVE QUICKLY FROM WIDE TO TIGHT VIEWS.

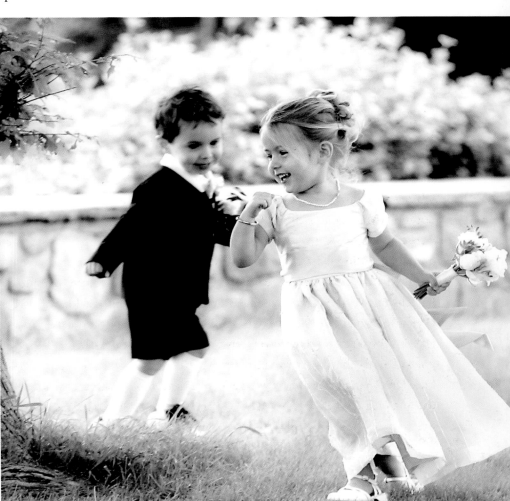

Long telephotos and telephoto zooms let you "cherry pick" priceless shots without being observed. Photograph by Dan Doke.

Wide Angles. Wide-angle lenses, both fixed focal length lenses and wide-angle zooms, are also popular. Focal lengths from 17mm to 35mm are ideal for capturing the atmosphere as well as for photographing larger groups. These lenses are fast enough for use by available light with fast ISOs.

Telephotos. Another favorite lens is the high-speed telephoto—the 400mm f/2.8 or 300mm f/4.0 (Nikon) and the 300mm and 400mm f/2.8L (Canon) lenses. These lenses are ideal for working unobserved and can isolate some wonderful moments, particularly of the ceremony. Even more than the 80–200mm lens, the 300mm or 400mm lenses throw backgrounds beautifully out of focus and, when used wide open, provide a sumptuously thin band of focus, which is ideal for isolating image details.

Another popular choice is the 85mm (f/1.2 for Canon; f/1.4 or f/1.8 for Nikon), which is a short telephoto with exceptional sharpness. This lens gets used frequently at receptions because of its speed and ability to throw backgrounds out of focus, depending on the subject-to-camera distance. It is one of Marcus Bell's preferred lenses for his wedding-day coverage.

LEFT—One of Nick Adams' favorite lenses is the AF NIKKOR 85mm f/1.4D IF. Its razor sharpness and thin band of focus blurs backgrounds into a smooth canvas of subtle tones. This image was made with a Nikon D2X and the 85mm f/1.4 used wide open. **RIGHT**—Michael Costa used a 50mm f/1.4 lens with his Canon EOS 5D to create this nighttime shot. He metered for the couple, not the bonfire in the background. You can find f/1.4 or even f/1.2 50mm lenses on the used lens market for a pittance.

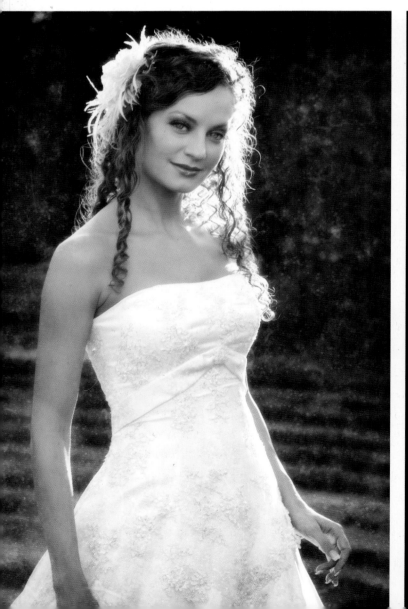

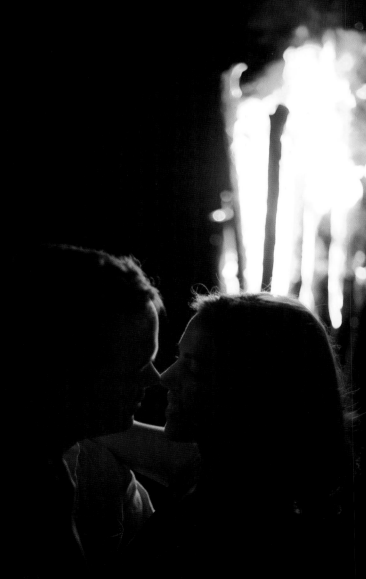

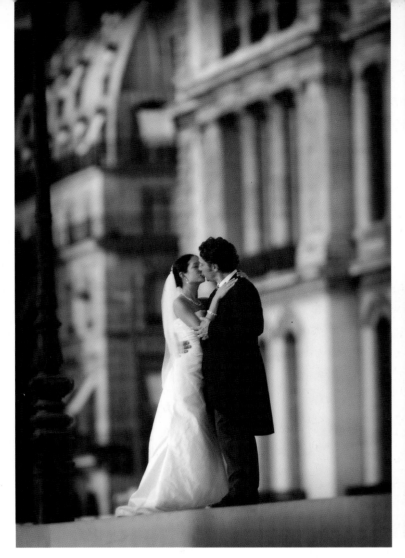

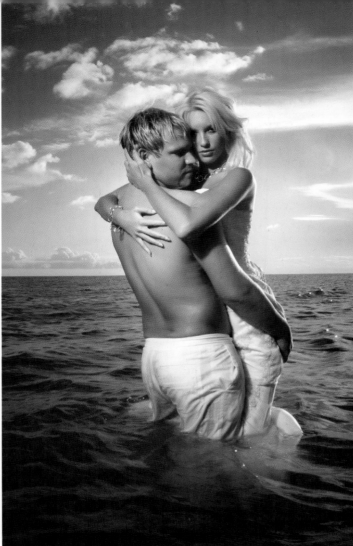

LEFT—Mike Colon used his Nikon D2X and AF-S VR NIKKOR 200mm f/2G IF-ED at f/2.0 to blur the background of the Venetian architecture. RIGHT—A wide-angle lens made the clouds and white caps in the background seem intimately close to the subjects. Kevin Jairaj made this image with a Canon EOS 5D and EF 16–35mm f/2.8L II USM lens at 16mm. He stopped the lens down to f/18 to increase depth of field, making the background elements seem even more relevant.

The Normal Lens. One should not, however, forget about the "normal" 50mm f/1.2 or f/1.4 lens for digital photography. With a 1.4x focal length factor, for example, that lens becomes a 70mm f/1.2 or f/1.4 lens that is ideal for portraits or groups, especially in low light. And the close-focusing distance of this lens makes it an extremely versatile wedding lens.

Perspective and Distortion. When selecting a lens, the perspective it provides should always be considered. Wide-angle lenses will distort the subject's appearance, particularly if they are close to the camera or near the edge of the frame. In group portraits, the subjects in the front row will appear larger than those in the back of the group, especially if you get too close. Even "normal" lenses (50mm in 35mm format, 75–90mm in the medium formats) tend to exaggerate subject features at closer working distances. Noses appear elongated, chins jut out, and the backs of heads may appear smaller than normal. This phenomenon is known as foreshortening. At longer working distances (such as when creating three-quarter-length portraits or group portraits), however, normal lenses are a good choice and will provide normal perspective.

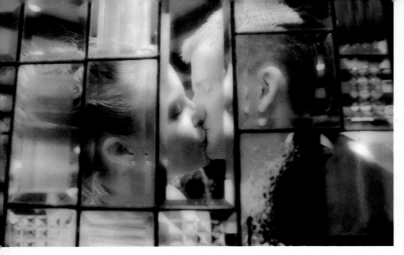

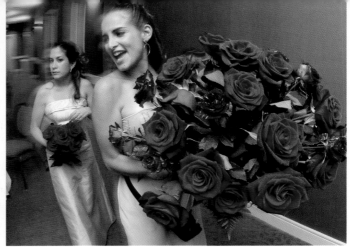

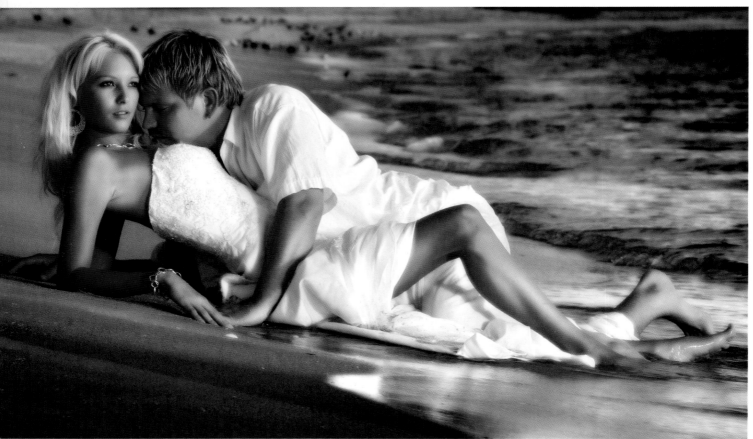

For close shots of individual subjects and couples, short to medium telephotos are a good choice. You can even use a much longer lens if you have the working room. A 200mm lens, for instance, is a beautiful portrait lens for the 35mm format because it provides very shallow depth of field and throws the background completely out of focus (when used at maximum aperture), providing a backdrop that won't distract viewers from the subject. Keep in mind, though, that very long lenses (300mm and longer for 35mm) can sometimes distort perspective unless used at awkwardly long camera-to-subject distances. If the working distance is too short, the subject's features appear compressed; the nose may appear pasted onto the sub-

TOP LEFT—David Beckstead loves his wide-angle zooms, which let him tie foreground elements (here, the leaded-glass window) into a closely cropped composition. **TOP RIGHT**—Jeff Kolodny fisheye lens to create a wonderful effect. Notice that the roses, very close to the lens, look huge, while other aspects of the scene recede in size quite dramatically. This is a normal fisheye effect. **ABOVE**—Telephoto lenses "stack" perspective, compressing the apparent distance of background elements. Photograph by Kevin Jairaj.

FOCAL-LENGTH FACTORS

Since all but full-frame DSLRs have chip sizes smaller than 24x36mm (the size of a 35mm film frame), there is a magnification factor that changes the effective focal length of the lens. For instance, Nikon DSLRs have a 1.5x focal-length factor that makes a 50mm lens function as a 75mm lens (50 x 1.5 = 75)—an ideal portrait lens.

Because digital lenses do not have to produce as wide a circle of coverage as lenses designed for full-frame (24x36mm) chips, lens manufacturers have been able to come up with some splendid long-range zooms that cover wide-angle to telephoto focal lengths. Lenses like Canon's EF 28–300mm f/3.5–5.6L IS USM and EF 28–200mm f/3.5–5.6 USM are fast, lightweight, and extremely versatile.

ject's face, and the ears may appear parallel to the eyes. These very long lenses are, however, ideal for working unobserved—you can make head-and-shoulders images from a long distance away.

10. GET THE EXPOSURE RIGHT

Accuracy is Critical. The wedding day presents the ultimate in exposure extremes (a black tuxedo and a white wedding dress), and when shooting digitally (especially JPEGs) the exposure latitude is virtually nonexistent. Underexposed digital files tend to have an excessive amount of noise; overexposed files lack image detail in the highlights. You must be right on with your exposures when shooting JPEGs. If you make an error, though, let it be in the direction of slight underexposure, which is survivable. Overexposure of any kind is a deal breaker. You must also guarantee that the dynamic range of the processed image fits that of the materials you will use to exhibit the image (i.e., the printing paper, ink, or photographic paper).

Meters. The preferred meter for portraits is the handheld incident light meter. This measures the amount of light falling on the scene (rather than the reflectance of the subjects) and yields extremely consistent results, because it is less likely to be influenced by highly reflective or light-absorbing surfaces. To use this meter, simply stand where you want your subjects to be, point the dome of the meter directly at the camera lens and take a reading. If you can't physically get to your subject's position, meter the light at your location (if it is the same as the lighting at the subject position).

A handheld incident flashmeter is also invaluable when using multiple strobes and when trying to determine the overall evenness of lighting in a large room.

Meter Calibration. Like all mechanical instruments, meters can get out of whack and need periodic adjustment to ensure accuracy. Therefore, it is advisable to run periodic checks on your handheld and in-camera meters; after all, you base the majority of your exposures on their data. If your in-

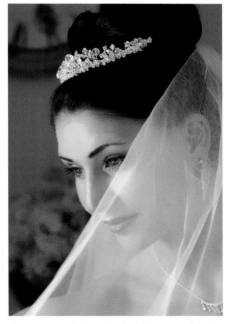

This is an window-light photograph of a bride taken before the ceremony. A gold Light Disc reflector was added for fill, and the camera's white balance was adjusted to create warmer flesh tones. Photograph by Michael O'Neill.

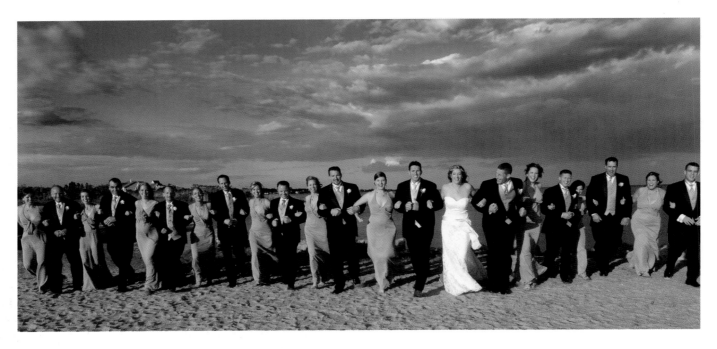

cident meter is also a flashmeter, you should check it against a second meter to verify its accuracy.

Quick Exposure Evaluation. There are two ways to quickly evaluate the exposure of the captured image. First, the LCD monitor provides a quick visual reference for making sure things are okay in terms of the sharpness and exposure. For more accurate feedback, however, you should review the histogram. This is a graphic representation of the number of pixels at each brightness level. The range of the histogram represents 0–255 from left to right, with 0 indicating "absolute" black and 255 indicating "absolute" white. In an image with a good range of tones, the histogram will fill the length of the graph and (in most cases) trail off on either end. When an exposure has detailed highlights, these will fall in the 235–245 range; when an image has detailed blacks, these will fall in the 15–30 range (RGB mode).

When creating this playful image of a huge bridal party on the beach, Michael O'Neill relied upon his Nikon D2X's 3D matrix metering, coupled with the Nikon SB-800's high-speed flash-sync capabilities to properly expose the scene while he concentrated on directing the group.

11. Choose the Right Shutter Speed

You must choose a shutter speed that stills both camera and subject movement. If using a tripod, a shutter speed of $\frac{1}{15}$ to $\frac{1}{60}$ second should be adequate to stop average subject movement. Outdoors, you should normally choose a shutter speed faster than $\frac{1}{60}$ second, because even a slight breeze will cause the subject's hair to flutter, producing motion during the moment of exposure. If you are using electronic flash, you are locked into the flash-sync speed your camera calls for unless you are dragging the shutter (working at a slower-than-flash-sync shutter speed to bring up the level of the ambient light).

When handholding the camera, you should select a shutter speed that is the reciprocal of the focal length of the lens you are using (or faster). For example, if using a 100mm lens, use $\frac{1}{100}$ second (or the next highest equivalent shutter speed, like $\frac{1}{125}$) under average conditions. Some photographers are able to handhold their cameras for impossibly long exposures, like $\frac{1}{4}$ or $\frac{1}{2}$ second. To do this, you must practice good breathing and shooting techniques. With the handheld camera laid flat in the palm of your hand and your elbows in against your body, take a deep breath and hold it. Do not exhale until you've squeezed the shutter. Spread your feet like a tripod and if you are near a doorway, lean against it for additional support.

MICHAEL O'NEILL ON EXPOSURE

According to Michael O'Neill, "My digital camera [a Nikon D2X] is set in the manual-exposure mode about 90 percent of the time. My camera does not know that it is a digital camera with awesome 3D Color Matrix metering capabilities. It does, however, know how to record a properly lit and exposed scene the same way my film cameras did. My trusty Minolta flashmeter still occupies a readily accessible spot in my camera bag and gets pulled out for ambient light or manual electronic flash readings many times throughout the wedding day. I usually start my day metering the light falling through an appropriate window at the bride's home for intimate available-light portraits of the bride, her parents and her bridesmaids. All of my ceremony shots are done in manual exposure mode and most are done pre-focused with the camera's autofocus capabilities turned off. Ditto for the candid shots at the reception."

The window-light photograph of the bride was taken before the ceremony with a gold Light Disc reflector fill. This was a manual exposure metered with a handheld incident-light meter. Manual white balance setting was used on the Nikon D2X to achieve the warm flesh tones. Photograph by Michael O'Neill.

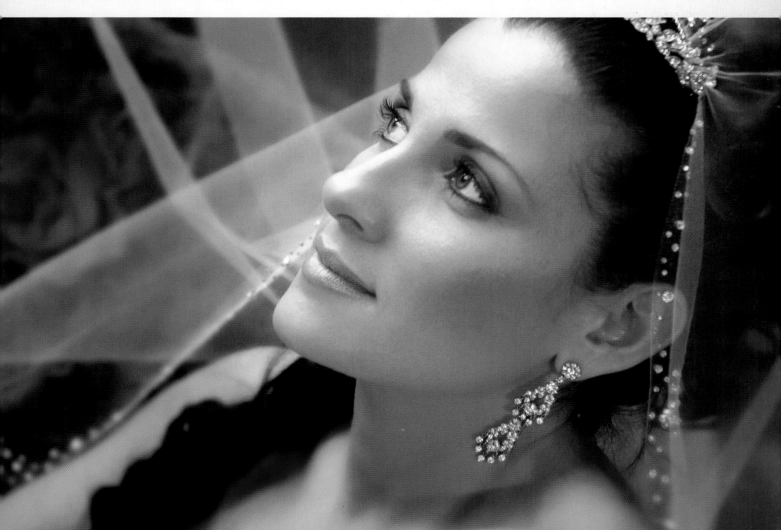

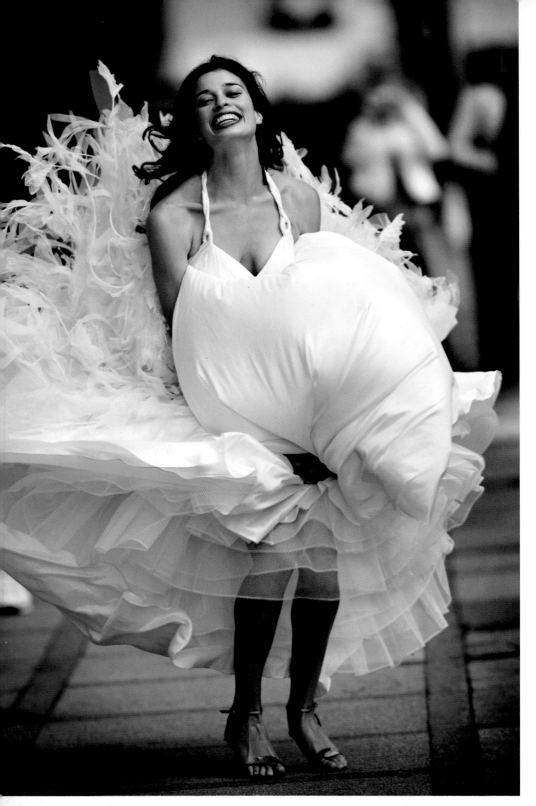

This is one of my all-time favorite wedding images. The photographer, Mike Colón, used an AF-S VR Nikkor 200mm f/2G IF-ED lens, which is astronomically expensive (with diamonds you pay for size [karats]; with lenses you pay for speed [f/2.0]). Naturally, Mike shoots wide open to exploit the very shallow depth of field and impeccable sharpness of this lens. With VR (vibration reduction) technology on board, he never has to worry about shutter speed.

YOU WILL NEED TO USE
A FASTER SHUTTER SPEED
BECAUSE OF THE INCREASED
IMAGE MAGNIFICATION.

If you are shooting handheld and working very close to the subjects, as you might be when making a portrait of a couple, you will need to use a faster shutter speed because of the increased image magnification. When working farther away from the subject, you can revert to the shutter speed that is the reciprocal of your lens's focal length. When shooting subjects in motion, use a faster shutter speed and a wider lens aperture. In this kind of shot, it's more important to freeze subject movement than it is to have great depth of field. Ultimately, if you have any question as to which speed to use, use the next fastest speed to ensure sharpness.

A great technical improvement is the development of image stabilization lenses, which correct for camera movement and allow you to shoot hand-held with long lenses and slower shutter speeds. Canon and Nikon, two companies that currently offer this feature in some of their lenses, offer a wide variety of zooms and long focal length lenses with image stabilization. If using a zoom, for instance, which has a maximum aperture of f/4, you can shoot handheld wide open in subdued light at $\frac{1}{10}$ or $\frac{1}{15}$ second and get dramatically sharp results. This means that you can use the natural light longer into the day while still shooting at low ISO settings for fine grain. It is important to note, however, that subject movement will not be quelled with these lenses, only camera movement.

> A GREAT TECHNICAL IMPROVEMENT IS THE DEVELOPMENT OF IMAGE STABILIZATION LENSES.

12. CHOOSE THE RIGHT APERTURE

The closer you are to your subjects, with any lens, the less depth of field you will have at any given aperture. When you are shooting a tight image of faces, be sure that you have enough depth of field at your working lens aperture to hold the focus on all the faces. At wide lens apertures, you will need to focus very carefully to keep the eyes, lips, and tip of the nose criti-cally sharp. This is where a good working knowledge of your lenses is es-sential. Some lenses will have the majority (two thirds) of their depth of

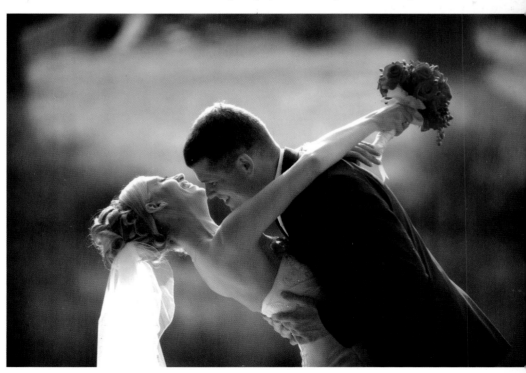

Laura Novak used a fast shutter speed to still the unpredictable motion of the bride and groom and a wide-open lens aperture of f/2.8 to de-emphasize the background, accenting the couple.

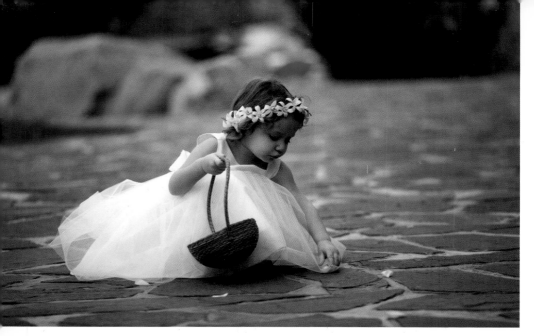

Joe Buissink made this charming image of a flower girl doing some last-minute housekeeping duties, with a 70–200mm lens at f/2.8. His focus is in sync with the storytelling aspects of the image. The face, hands, and basket of the little girl are all in focus, but nothing else is, so that the impact of the image derives from its significant elements. Depth of focus entails knowing exactly where to place the point of sharp focus so that the details convey the intended message.

field behind the point of focus; others will have the majority (two thirds) of their depth of field in front of the point of focus. In most cases, depth of field is split 50–50, half in front of and half behind the point of focus.

You should also learn to use the magnification function on your LCD back to inspect the depth-of-field of your images. The viewfinder screen is often too dim to gauge overall image sharpness accurately when the lens is stopped down with the depth-of-field preview. Double-checking the focus on your LCD will help ensure you got the sharpness you wanted.

13. SELECT THE OPTIMAL COLOR SPACE

Many DSLRs allow you to shoot in the Adobe RGB 1998 or sRGB color space. There is considerable confusion over which is the "right" choice. Adobe RGB 1998 is a wider gamut color space than sRGB, so many photographers reason that this is the best option. Professional digital-imaging labs, however, use sRGB for their digital printers. Therefore, photographers working in Adobe 1998 RGB may be somewhat disheartened when their files are reconfigured and output in the narrower sRGB color space. As a result, many photographers use the Adobe 1998 RGB color space right up to the point that files are sent to a printer or out to the lab for printing.

Is there ever a need for other color spaces? Yes. It depends on your particular workflow. For example, all the images you see in this book have been converted from their native sRGB or Adobe 1998 RGB color space to the CMYK color space for photomechanical printing. As a general preference, I prefer images from photographers be in the Adobe 1998 RGB color space, as they seem to convert more naturally to CMYK.

In Adobe Camera Raw and other RAW-file processing software there exists another color space, which has become quite popular, called ProPhoto RGB. It is a "sticky" color space, meaning that it adds color data

IS THERE EVER A NEED FOR OTHER COLOR SPACES? YES. IT DEPENDS ON YOUR PARTICULAR WORKFLOW.

to the file. The added data cannot be seen on monitors currently sold, but what *can* be seen is the increased resolution and size of the image file. A typical RAW file made with a Nikon D200, which uses a 10.2MP sensor, produces a file in the neighborhood of 22 or 23MB. A good size file, to be sure—but when ProPhoto RGB is used to process the image in the RAW file processor, the file opens at 72MB, a very healthy increase in file size and potential resolution. Many photographers who shoot RAW, and also make large prints, process the images in this color space to take advantage of the added color data and larger file sizes.

14. THE WHITE BALANCE SAVES TIME

Choosing the right white-balance setting is particularly important if you are shooting JPEG files; it is less important when shooting in the RAW file mode, since these files contain more data than JPEGs and allow color imbalances to be easily remedied in postproduction. While this would seem to argue for shooting exclusively RAW files, it's important to note that these files take up more room on media cards and require more time to write to the cards. As a result, many wedding photographers find it more practical to shoot JPEGs and perfect the color balance when creating the exposure.

A system that many pros follow is to take a custom white balance of a scene where they are unsure of the lighting mix. By selecting a white area

Ray Prevost created this untraditional bridal portrait to show the differences between the bride and groom, something he feels are as much a part of marriage as any other factor. In this case, the couple had both a traditional Sikh wedding and a Western wedding and reception. Ray used a "shady" white-balance setting on his Canon 20D. For the main light he used a Vivitar 285, Quantum Battery 1+, Litedome Q39 softbox, and Quantum Radio Slave 4i.

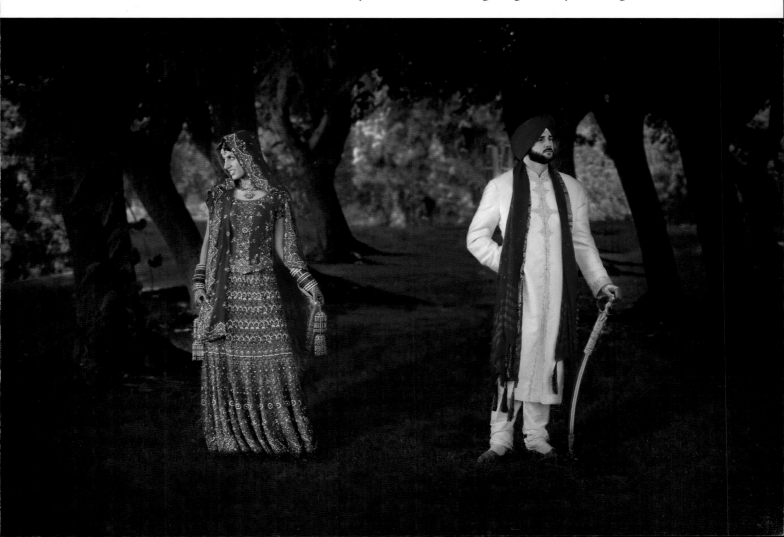

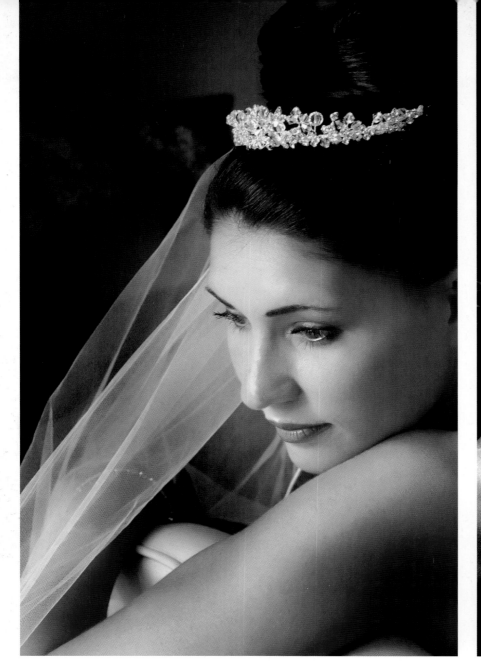

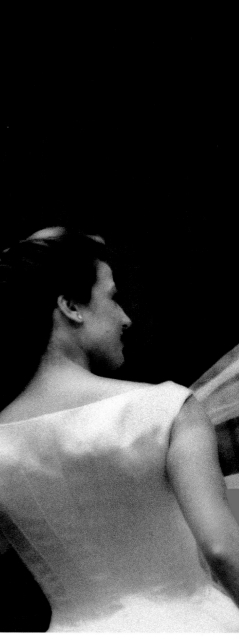

in the scene and neutralizing it with a custom white-balance setting, you can be assured of an accurate color rendition. Others swear by a device known as the ExpoDisc (www.expodisc.com), which attaches to the the lens like a filter and is highly accurate in most situations .

15. Watch Your ISO Settings

In general, the higher the ISO setting on your camera, the more noise will be recorded. This is a condition, akin to visible grain in film photography, that occurs in digital imaging when stray electronic information affects the sensor sites. Fortunately, this is less of a problem than it once was. At this writing, the latest pro DSLRs from Nikon (D3) and Canon (EOS 1Ds Mark III) feature remarkably high ISOs and low noise. Nikon's D3 even of-

LEFT—This is a window-light photograph of the bride taken before the ceremony with a gold Light Disc reflector used for fill. The camera's white-balance setting was adjusted to create warmer flesh tones. Photograph by Michael O'Neill.

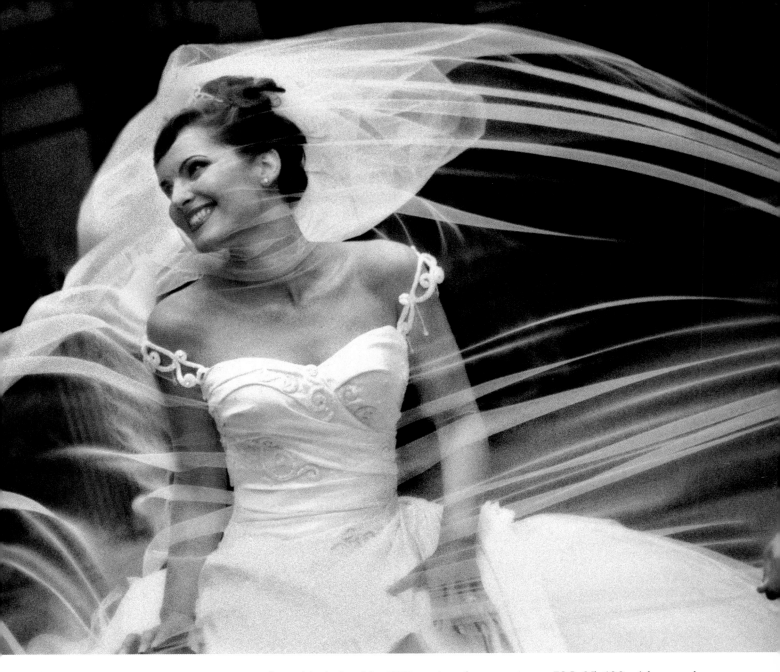

ABOVE—This image by Yervant was shot with available light on a windy and overcast day. The bride's veil was a very light silk and kept flying in the wind. Yervant copied sections of the image to make a new layer (the veil). Once he had the new layer, he then added motion blur (Filter> Blur) in Photoshop in the direction of the veil's natural flow to boost the life in the moment. He then selected a section of the background and applied the purple hue to make it less tonally demanding. After he flattened the image, he added a bit of grain (Filter>Texture>Grain) to make the image suit his own personal taste.

fers a black & white ISO setting that goes up to ISO 25,600 with remarkably low noise. Many DSLRs also feature specialized modes that automatically reduce noise in long-exposure situations. These settings are quite effective, regardless of ISO.

There are also a number of effective noise-reducing applications available for postproduction. Adobe Camera Raw features two types of noise reduction (one for color noise [chrominance] and one for black & white noise [luminance]) that can be applied in RAW file processing. Nik Software's dFine 2.0 is another very sophisticated noise-reduction program that lets you reduce noise globally or selectively, targeting critical parts of the image.

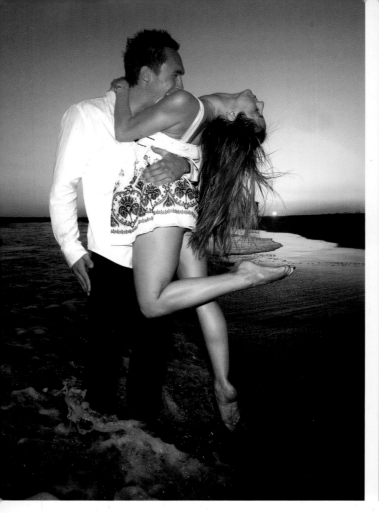

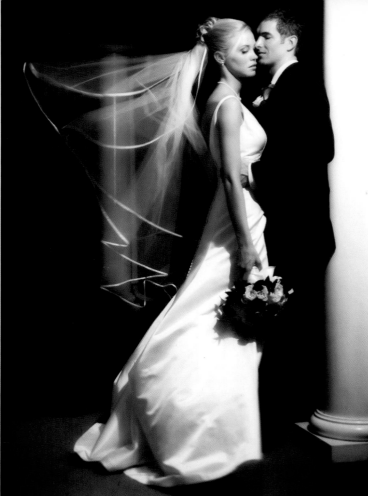

16. FILE FORMAT: SPEED VS. VERSATILITY

RAW Files. RAW files retain the highest amount of image data from the original capture, so the files can be "fixed" to a much greater degree than JPEG files. However, if you are like most wedding photographers and need fast burst rates, RAW files will likely slow you down. RAW files will also fill up your storage cards much more quickly because of their larger file size. (*Note:* Because camera buffers and processing speeds have increased in size and performance, increasing numbers of professional wedding photographers are opting to shoot RAW files. If you know a situation is coming where you will need fast burst rates, you can always switch temporarily to the JPEG fine mode, and then back to RAW when the moment passes.)

Shooting in the RAW mode also requires the use of file-processing software to translate the file data into a useable format. This adds another step to your postproduction workflow, but provides valuable control over white balance, tint, exposure, brightness, contrast, saturation, luminance smoothing, color noise reduction, chromatic aberration, vignetting, tone curve (contrast control), shadow tint, and red, green, and blue saturation.

JPEG. Your other option is to shoot in the JPEG Fine mode (sometimes called JPEG Highest Quality). This creates smaller files, so you can

LEFT—Ben Chen is an accomplished sports photographer turned wedding photographer. He shot this image in RAW and adjusted the color temperature, tint, shadows, brightness, contrast, sharpness, color noise reduction, and used a medium contrast tone curve. **RIGHT**—Kevin Jairaj created this beautiful portrait of a bride and groom for print competition. Kevin often shoots in the RAW format so he can adjust the skin tones and lighting subtleties after the capture. In this image, he used a single flash to light the couple and had an assistant "drop" the veil an instant before exposure so it would look like it was suspended in mid air.

Adobe DNG Format

To resolve the disparity between the many proprietary RAW file formats (most camera manufacturer's have their own format), Adobe Systems introduced an open RAW file format called the Digital Negative (DNG) format and is encouraging digital camera manufacturers and software developers to adopt the standard. Unlike many existing RAW formats, DNG was designed with enough built-in flexibility to incorporate all the image data and metadata that a digital camera might generate. Currently, proprietary RAW file format images that are pulled into Photoshop (CS2 and above) can be saved to the DNG file format with all the RAW file format characteristics retained. You can also embed the original RAW file in the saved DNG file, convert the image data to an interpolated format, and vary the compression ratio of the accompanying JPEG preview image.

save more images per media card and work much more quickly. Because of this increased speed and flexibility, many pros shoot in the JPEG Fine mode. Because there is less data preserved in this format, however, your exposure and white balance must be flawless. In short, the JPEG format is efficient, but it will reveal any weakness in your technique. (*Note:* Because the JPEG format compresses file information, the files are subject to degradation by repeated saving. If you shoot in JPEG mode, save your working copy of the file in the TIFF format [see page 42].)

[see page 42]

BECAUSE THERE IS LESS DATA PRESERVED IN THIS FORMAT, YOUR EXPOSURE AND WHITE BALANCE MUST BE FLAWLESS.

Other Useful Formats. The JPEG 2000 format (supported by an option plug-in in Photoshop) provides more options and greater flexibility than the standard JPEG format. It offers optional lossless compression as well as 16-bit color/grayscale files, 8-bit transparency, and both alpha and spot channels can be saved. A very interesting feature of the JPEG 2000 format is that it supports using a Region of Interest (ROI) to minimize file size and preserve quality in critical areas of an image. By using an alpha channel, you can specify the region (ROI) where the most detail should be preserved, minimizing the compression (and loss of detail) in that area.

GIF (Graphics Interchange Format) is a file format commonly used to display indexed-color graphics and images in hypertext markup language (HTML) documents over the Internet. GIF is an LZW-compressed format

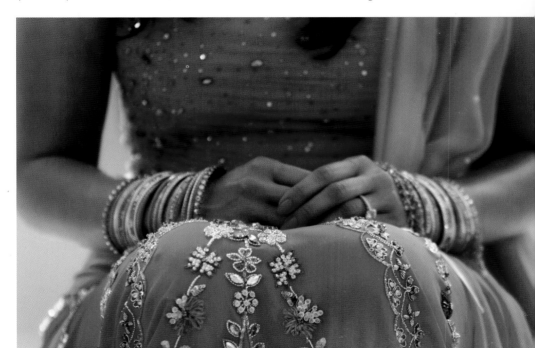

Even wedding images that were originally recorded in RAW capture mode are often converted to JPEGs for uploading and printing. Photograph by Mark Cafeiro.

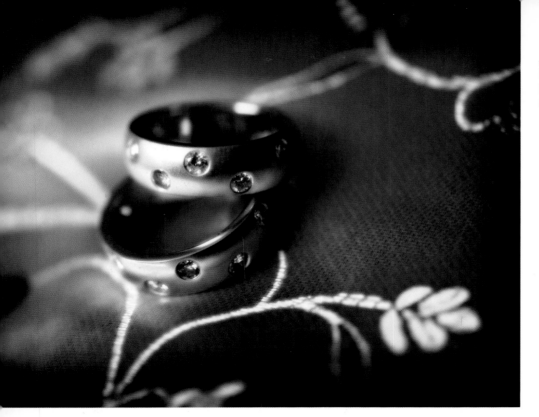

A close-up detail shot of the rings should be on every photographer's shot list. Brides especially want this shot in the album. Photograph by Tamara Lackey.

designed to minimize file size and electronic transfer time. The GIF format preserves transparency in indexed-color images; however, it does not support alpha channels.

TIFF (Tagged Image File Format) files are lossless, meaning that they do not degrade in image quality when repeatedly opened and closed. This is a very flexible image format supported by virtually all painting, image-editing, and page-layout applications. Also, virtually all desktop scanners can produce TIFF files. Photoshop can save layers in a TIFF file; however, if you open the file in another application, only the flattened image is visible. Photoshop can also save annotations, transparency, and multi-resolution pyramid data in TIFF format.

PSD (Photoshop Document) is Photoshop's native file format and the only format that supports most Photoshop features (other than the Large Document Format [PSB]). Due to the tight integration between Adobe products, other Adobe applications can directly import PSD files and preserve many Photoshop features. Saving a PSD file is worthwhile if complicated manipulations were performed in Photoshop; in the File Info section of a PSD file, all of the procedures will be documented in chronological order.

LOSSLESS FORMATS COMPRESS THE FILE WITHOUT REMOVING IMAGE DETAIL OR COLOR INFORMATION.

17. WATCH THE FILE COMPRESSION

Many file formats use compression to reduce file size. Lossless formats compress the file without removing image detail or color information. Lossy formats remove detail. Here are some common compression schemes:

LZW. LZW is a lossless compression strategy supported by TIFF, PDF, GIF, and PostScript language file formats. It provides the greatest reduction in file size when used for images that contain large areas of a single color.

JPEG. JPEG is a lossy compression strategy supported by JPEG, TIFF, PDF, and PostScript language file formats. When saving an image in the JPEG format in Photoshop, you can specify the level of compression by choosing an option from the Quality menu (in the JPEG Options dialog box). For the best results, always choose the highest image quality (a setting of 10 to 12).

ZIP. ZIP is a lossless compression strategy that is supported by PDF and TIFF file formats. Like LZW, the ZIP compression strategy provides the greatest reduction in file size when used for images containing large areas of a single color.

18. CHIMPING: EVALUATING AN IMAGE

The term "chimping" is attributed to *USA Today* sports photographer Robert Deutsch, who used it to describe the scene of multiple digital photographers, covering the 1999 US Open, simultaneously checking their LCDs after each backhand (as he writes, "all looking at their screens like monkeys").

While the concept of "chimping" certainly has a derogatory feel to it, the practice of checking your LCD can be very useful. With higher resolution LCDs, larger screens, and more functions in the playback mode of the camera, there's no reason you can't use the LCD most of the time for evaluating images. For example, most professional DSLRs let you zoom and scroll across an image at high magnification to evaluate details. This will tell you if the image is sharp or not.

THERE'S NO REASON YOU CAN'T USE THE LCD MOST OF THE TIME FOR EVALUATING IMAGES.

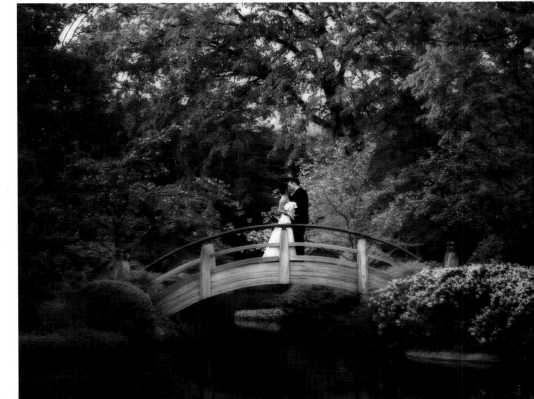

The JPEG format allows the photographer to work quickly and conserve storage space. This file, when closed, is 1.47MB as a JPEG. Once opened, it is a 20.60MB file. Once transported or sent to another party, files like these should be saved as lossless TIFF files to preserve the image data. This beautiful bridal formal was made by Kevin Jairaj.

Also, you can set certain playback presets to automatically indicate problems like clipped highlights (bright regions of the image in which no detail is present). With this feature, the clipped highlights blink on the LCD preview, so you can tell what areas were not properly exposed and how to remedy the situation. On Nikon's playback menu, you can switch from histogram back to highlight-clipping mode in an instant. As you begin to use these features, they become second nature to your shooting workflow.

19. UNDERSTAND POSING ESSENTIALS

No matter what style of photography is being used, there are certain posing essentials that need to be at work—otherwise your technique (or lack of it) will be obvious. The more you know about the rules of posing, and particularly the subtleties, the more you can apply to your wedding images. And the more you practice these principles, the more they will become second nature and a part of your overall technique.

Giving Directions. There are a number of ways to give posing instructions. You can tell your subjects what you want them to do, you can gently move them into position, or you can demonstrate the pose. The latter is perhaps the most effective, as it breaks down barriers of self-consciousness on both sides of the camera.

Subject Comfort. A subject who feels uncomfortable will most likely look uncomfortable in the photos. After all, these are normal people, not

LEFT—Here is classically elegant head-and-shoulders portrait by Michael Schuhmann. At first glance, the portrait looks very symmetrical, but on closer inspection you'll see that there are numerous diagonal and curved lines, plus the pleasant line of the hands cupping her face. Notice, too, that the bride's hands are not pressing against her cheeks, which would distort her face; they are barely touching the skin. That's a good posing tip when hands are included in a head-and-shoulders portrait. **RIGHT**—Good posing skills are acquired over time and with diligence. Dan Doke made this charming portrait of his bride on location. Notice how the eyes are at a slight angle, the head tipped toward the near shoulder, and the fingers slightly separated—all important posing techniques.

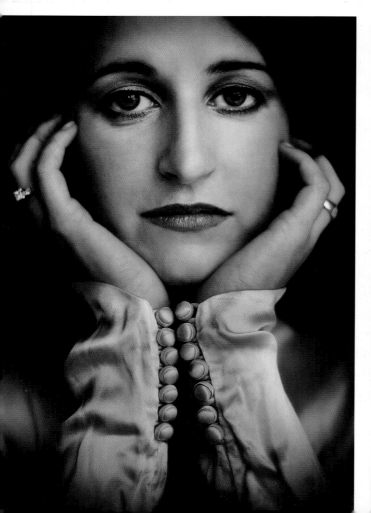

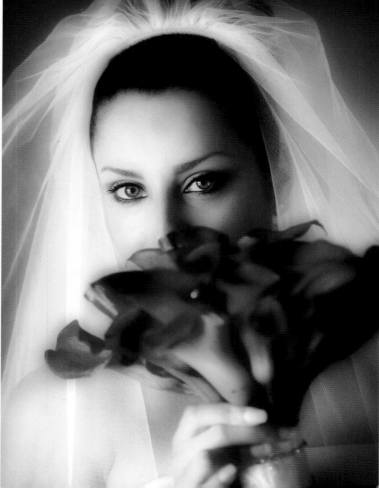

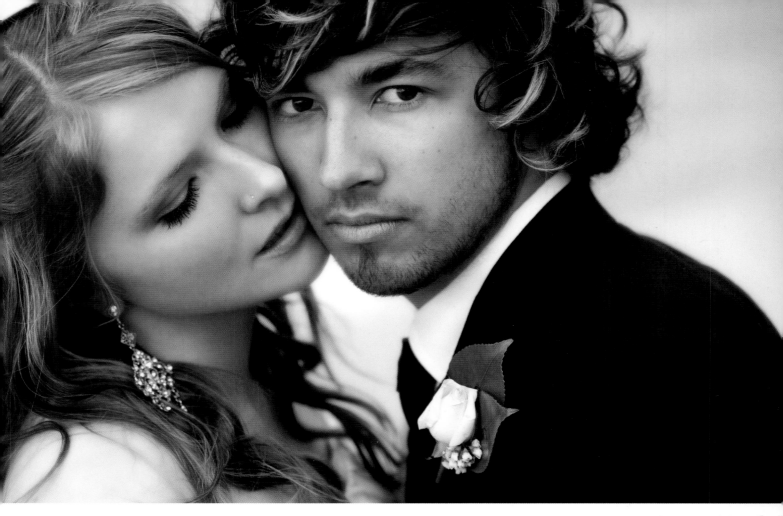

Australian wedding photographer Jerry Ghionis thinks of himself more as a director than a photographer who issues posing commands. He believes that by acting out the pose (showing rather than talking about it) he gets better cooperation—and he's not afraid to look silly acting out the poses if it leads to a great image.

models who make their living posing. Use a pose that feels good to the subject, then use your expertise to refine it—add a turn of a wrist, place the weight on the back foot, turn the body away from the camera—to create the most flattering look possible.

20. CHOOSE A PORTRAIT LENGTH

Head and Shoulders. In a head-and-shoulders portrait, all of your camera technique will be evident, so focus is critical (start with the eyes) and the lighting must be flawless. Use changes in camera height to correct any irregularities. Often, head-and-shoulders portraits are of the face alone—as in a beauty shot. In such an image, it is important to have a dynamic element, like a diagonal line, to create visual interest. This can be the line of the eyes, the tilt of the head, or the line of the shoulders.

Three-Quarter and Full-Length Poses. When you employ a three-quarter-length pose (showing the subject from the head to below the waist) or a full-length pose (showing the subject from head to toe), you have more of the body to contend with.

In these types of portraits, it is important to turn the body so that it is at an angle to the lens. Don't photograph the person head-on, as this adds

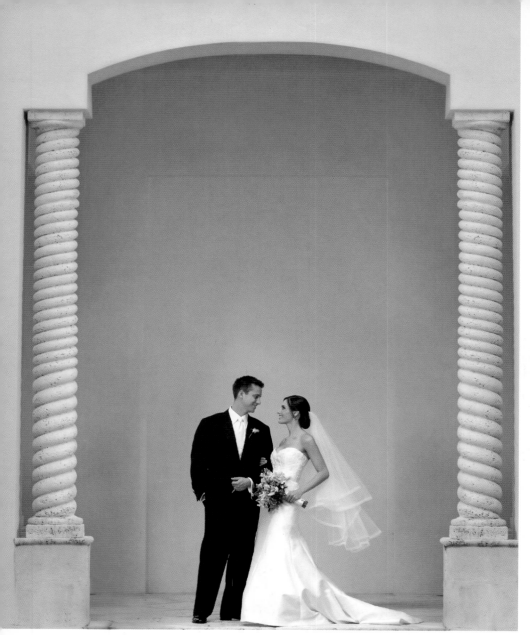

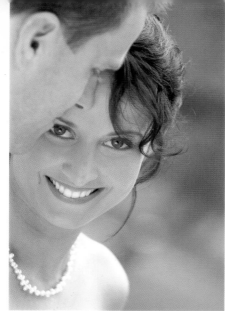

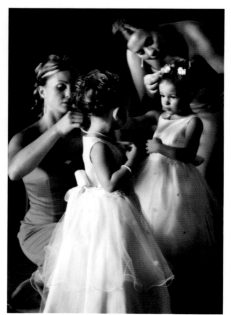

mass to the body. Also, your subject's weight should be on their back foot (the foot farthest from the camera) rather than distributed evenly on both feet—or, worse yet, on the front foot. There should be a slight bend in the front knee if the person is standing. This helps break up the static line of a straight leg. The feet should also be at an angle to the camera; feet look stumpy when shot straight on.

When the subject is sitting, a cross-legged pose is effective. Have the top leg facing at an angle and not directly into the lens. When posing a woman who is seated, have her tuck the calf of the leg closest to the camera in behind the leg farthest from the camera. This reduces the size of the calves, since the leg that is farther from the camera becomes more prominent. Whenever possible, have a slight space between the subject's leg and the chair, as this will slim down the thighs and calves.

LEFT—Great posing is evident in this image by Tom Muñoz. Here are some things to look at: weight on the back foot (both); bend in the forward knee (both); hand slightly out of pocket showing cuff for good tonal separation (groom); great posture, elbow out from the body, bouquet at waist height (bride); good hands with separation between fingers (both). Top it off with great expressions and you have an award-winning image. **TOP RIGHT**—Annika Metsla created this charming portrait, which is really of the bride (the groom only serves to lead the eye toward the bride). **BOTTOM RIGHT**—With minor direction and good point of view and lighting, Kevin Jairaj created a priceless image in which all aspects look normal and natural.

In three-quarter images, you should never frame the portrait so that a joint—an elbow, knee, or ankle, for example—is cut off at the edge of the frame. This sometimes happens when a portrait is cropped. Instead, crop between joints, at mid-thigh or mid-calf, for example. When you break the composition at a joint, it produces a disquieting feeling.

21. REFINE THE HEAD-AND-SHOULDERS AXIS

One of the basics of flattering portraiture is that the subject's shoulders should be turned at an angle to the camera. With the shoulders facing the camera straight on to the lens, the person looks wider than he or she really is. Additionally, the head should be turned in a different direction than the shoulders. This provides an opposing or complementary line within the photograph that, when seen together with the line of the body, creates a sense of tension and balance. With men, the head is often turned the same general direction as the shoulders (but not at exactly the same angle); with women, the head is usually at an angle that opposes the line of the body.

22. CONSIDER THE FACIAL VIEWS

As mentioned previously, the head should be at a different angle than the shoulders. There are three basic head positions (relative to the camera) found in portraiture: the seven-eighths view, the three-quarter view, and the profile view. Knowing these positions will help you provide variety in your images. In group portraits, you may even end up using all three head positions in a single pose (the more people in the group, the more likely that becomes).

The Seven-Eighths View. If you consider the full face as a head-on "mug shot," then the seven-eighths view is when the subject's face is turned just slightly away from the camera. In other words, you will see slightly more of one side of the subject's face. You will still see the subject's far ear in a seven-eighths view.

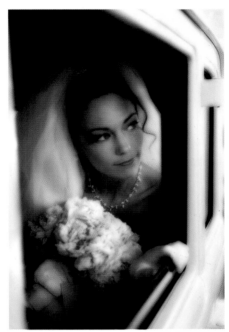

One of the vitals of good posing technique is to have the head turned or tilted at a different angle than the shoulders. Even in this "grab shot," you can see the ingredients of good posing. The bride's head is turned at a considerable angle to the almost straight-on shoulders. The reason for this guideline is to introduce a dynamic line into the composition that contrasts the line of the shoulders. Photograph by Jeff Hawkins.

Marc Weisberg created this head-and-shoulders portrait with an 85mm f/1.2 lens used wide open. The 85mm lens on a DSLR provides perfect perspective for head-and-shoulders portraits. To accent the bridesmaid's incredible blue eyes, Marc raised the camera so that it would be parallel to her eyes. This is a seven-eighths view of the face.

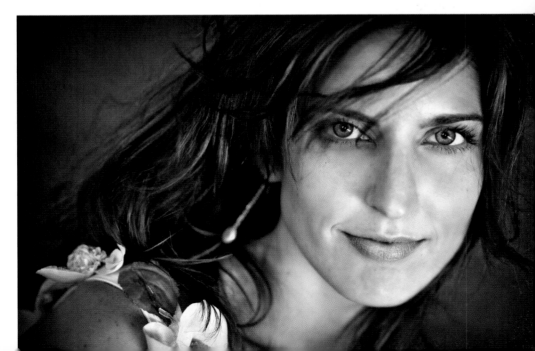

The Three-Quarter View. This view is achieved when the face is turned sufficiently that the far ear is hidden from the camera. With this pose, the far eye will appear smaller because it is farther away from the camera than the near eye. Because of this, it is important to position the subject so that their smaller eye (people usually have one eye that is slightly smaller than the other) is closest to the camera. This way, the perspective makes both eyes appear to be the same size in the photograph. This may not be something you have time to do when posing groups of people at a wedding, but when photographing the bride and groom, care should be taken to notice these subtleties.

Profile. In the profile, the head is turned almost 90 degrees to the camera. Only one eye is visible. In posing your subjects in profile, have them turn their heads gradually away from the camera position until the far eye and eyelashes just disappear.

23. WATCH THE EYES AND SMILE

The Eyes. The best way to keep your subject's eyes active and alive is to engage them in conversation. Look at the person while you are setting up and try to find a common frame of interest. Inquire about the other person—almost everyone loves to talk about themselves! If the person does not look at you when you are talking, he or she is either uncomfortable or shy. In either case, you have to work to relax the person. Try a variety of conversational topics until you find one he or she warms to and then pursue it. As you gain their interest, you will take the subject's mind off of the photograph. One of the best ways to enliven your subject's eyes is to tell an amusing story. If they enjoy it, their eyes will smile—one of the most endearing expressions a human being can make.

Start the formal session by having the person look at you. Using a cable release with the camera tripod-mounted forces you to become the host and allows you to physically hold the subject's gaze. It is a good idea to shoot a few frames of the person looking directly into the camera, but most people will appreciate some variety.

The Smile. One of the easiest ways to produce a natural smile is to praise your subject. Tell her how good she looks and how much you like a certain feature of hers—her eyes, her hair style, etc. To simply say "Smile!" will produce that familiar lifeless expression. By sincere confidence building and flattery, you will get the person to smile naturally and sincerely and their eyes will be engaged by what you are saying.

Remind the subject to moisten her lips periodically. This makes the lips sparkle in the finished portrait, as the moisture produces tiny specular highlights on the lips. Also, pay close attention to your subject's mouth, making sure there is no tension in the muscles around it, since this will give the

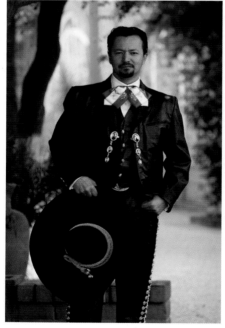

Here is an uncharacteristic pose made by Ken Sklute that seems to break all the rules, however, it is a highly effective portrait of the groom in traditional Mexican horseman's attire. Ken wanted to capture the strength and dignity of his groom and did so by making him face the camera head-on. Ken is a master at putting his subjects at ease and getting the most of their expressions.

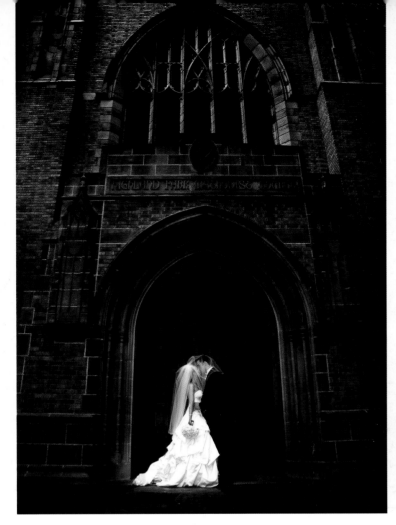

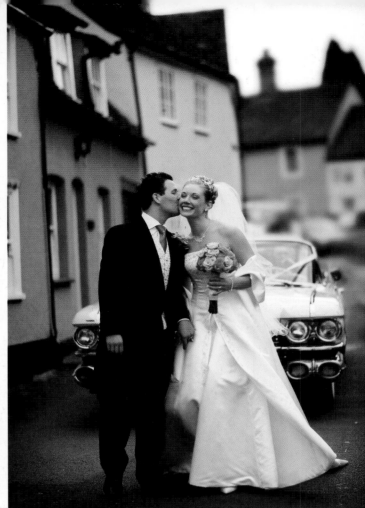

LEFT—Kevin Jairaj made this formal portrait of bride and groom kissing. Believe it or not, the bride and groom rarely get to kiss on their wedding day because they are so busy with other things. Kevin had the groom clutch the bride's waist and the bride drop her bouquet, as if overwhelmed by the kiss. He used a 17mm lens and fired a flash from camera position, and in Photoshop, gave the church exterior a blue-black treatment. **RIGHT**—A great smile resonates throughout the wedding album. Here British photographer Steve Tarling captured a priceless smile—along with a pink Cadillac—in a priceless wedding portrait. The spontaneity and joy in the shot is contagious.

portrait an unnatural, posed look. Again, an air of relaxation best relieves tension, so talk to the person to take his or her mind off the photo.

One of the best photographers I've ever seen at "enlivening" total strangers is Ken Sklute. I've looked at literally hundreds of his wedding images and in almost every photograph, the people are happy and relaxed in a natural, typical way. Nothing ever looks posed in his photography—it's almost as if he happened by this beautiful picture and snapped the shutter. One of the ways he gets people "under his spell" is with his enthusiasm for the excitement of the day; it's contagious and his affability translates into attentive subjects. While it helps any wedding photographer to be able to relate well to people, those with special gifts—good storytellers or a great sense of humor—should use those skills to get the most from their clients.

24. EVALUATE THE ARMS AND HANDS

Arms. Subjects' arms should generally not be allowed to fall to their sides, but should project outward to provide gently sloping lines and a "base" to the composition. This is achieved in a number of ways. For men, ask them to put their hands in their pockets; for women, ask them to bring their hands to their waist (whether they are seated or standing). Remind them

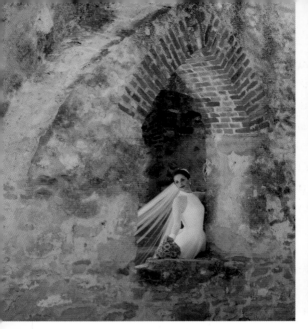

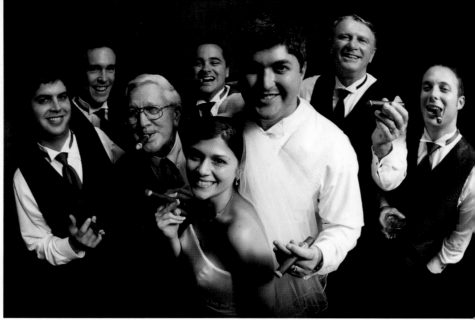

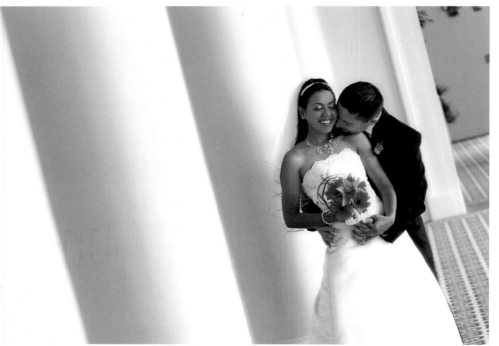

that there should be a slight space between their upper arms and their torsos. This triangular base in the composition visually attracts the viewer's eye upward, toward the face, and also prevents subjects from appearing to have flat and flabby arms.

Hands. Posing hands properly can be very difficult because, in most portraits, they are closer to the camera than the subject's head and thus appear larger. One thing that will give hands a more natural perspective is to use a longer-than-normal lens. Although holding the focus on both the hands and face is more difficult with a longer lens, the size relationship between them will appear more natural. If the hands are slightly out of focus, this is not as crucial as when the eyes or face are soft.

One basic rule is never to photograph a subject's hands pointing straight into the camera lens. This distorts the size and shape of the hands. Always have the hands at an angle to the lens. Another basic is to photograph the outer edge of the hand whenever possible. This gives a natural, flowing line to the hand and wrist and eliminates distortion that occurs when the hand is photographed from the top or head-on. Try to raise the wrist slightly so there is a gently curving line where the wrist and hand join. Additionally, you should always try to photograph the fingers with a slight separation in between them. This gives them form and definition. When the fingers are closed, there is no definition.

Hands can be a particular problem in group portraits. Despite their small size, they attract attention—especially against dark clothes. They can be especially troublesome in seated groups, where at first glance you might think there are more hands than there should be for the number of people pictured. A general rule of thumb is to either show all of the hand or show none of it. Don't allow a thumb or half a hand or only a few fingers to show. Hide as many hands as you can behind flowers, hats, or other people. Be aware of these potentially distracting elements and look for them as part of your visual inspection of the frame before you make the exposure.

25. Put the Weight on the Back Foot

The basic rule of thumb is that no one should be standing at attention with both feet together. Instead, the shoulders should be at a slight angle to the camera, as previously described, and the front foot should be brought forward slightly. The subject's weight should always be on the back foot. This has the effect of creating a bend in the front knee and dropping the rear shoulder to a position lower than the forward one. When used in full-length

TRY TO RAISE THE WRIST SLIGHTLY SO THERE IS A GENTLY CURVING LINE WHERE THE WRIST AND HAND JOIN.

Kevin Jairaj made this lovely portrait of the bride and her bridesmaids. The posing adheres to the fundamentals—weight on the back foot, elbows away from the body, show the edge of the hands, etc. But there is a little cockiness in each of the poses, which is in contrast to the very formal church arches. It's a good example of a quirky but fun formal portrait.

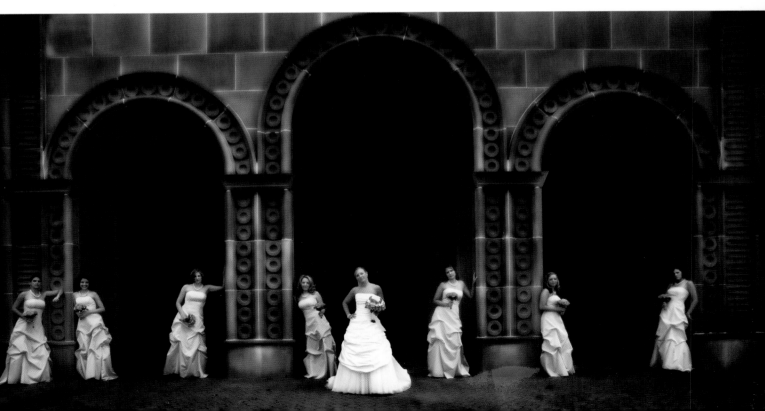

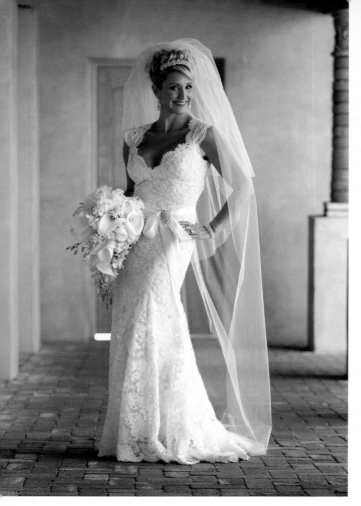

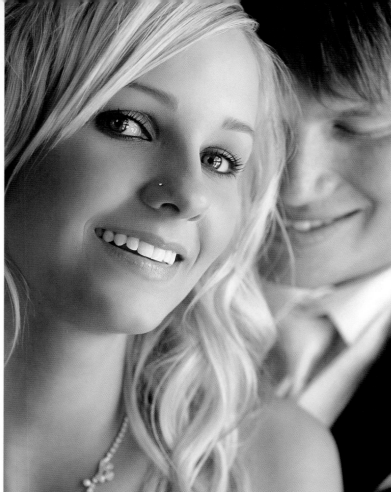

bridal portraits, a bent forward knee will lend an elegant shape to the dress. With one statement, "Weight on your back foot, please," you can introduce a series of dynamic lines into an otherwise average composition.

26. CONTROL THE CAMERA HEIGHT

When photographing people with average features, there are a few general rules that govern camera height in relation to the subject. These rules will produce normal (not exaggerated) perspective.

For head-and-shoulders portraits, the rule of thumb is that camera height should be the same height as the tip of the subject's nose. For three-quarter-length portraits, the camera should be at a height midway between the subject's waist and neck. In full-length portraits, the camera should be the same height as the subject's waist. In each case, the camera is at a height that divides the subject into two equal halves in the viewfinder. This is so that the features above and below the lens–subject axis will be the same distance from the lens, and thus recede equally for "normal" perspective.

When the camera is raised or lowered, the perspective (the size relationship between parts of the photo) changes. This is particularly exaggerated with wide-angle lenses. By controlling perspective, you can alter the subject's physical traits.

LEFT—This glamorous pose created by Ken Sklute handles all of the essential posing requirements, from head and shoulder axis, to the weight on the back foot, to photographing the edge of the hand. While it is formal and structured, it still looks like a relaxed pose, and shows off this elegant bride at her finest. **RIGHT**—While there are basic guidelines for camera height in order to satisfy perspective parameters, top photographers will often impose on those guidelines for a different effect. Here, Marc Weisberg lowered the camera height in this head-and-shoulders portrait to below the bride's chin, making her appear higher than the camera. It is a subtle adjustment that enhances the young bride's elegance and graceful neck.

By raising the camera height in a three-quarter- or full-length portrait, you enlarge the head-and-shoulders region of the subject, but slim the hips and legs. Conversely, lowering the camera reduces the size of the head, but enlarges the legs and thighs. Tilting the camera down when raising the camera (and up when lowering it) increases these effects. Also, the closer the camera is to the subject, the more pronounced the changes are. If you find that, after you adjust camera height for a desired effect, there is no change, move the camera in closer to the subject and observe the effect again.

When you raise or lower the camera in a head-and-shoulders portrait, the effects are even more dramatic. Raising the camera height lengthens the nose, narrows the chin and jaw line, and broadens the forehead. Lowering camera height shortens the nose, de-emphasizes the forehead, and widens the jaw line, while accentuating the chin.

> RAISING THE CAMERA HEIGHT LENGTHENS THE NOSE, NARROWS THE CHIN AND JAW LINE, AND BROADENS THE FOREHEAD.

While there is little time for many such corrections on the wedding day, knowing these rules and introducing them into the way you photograph people will help make the techniques second nature.

27. POSING COUPLES

The simplest of groups is one with just two people. Whether it's a bride and groom, mom and dad, or the best man and maid of honor, the basic building blocks call for one person slightly higher than the other. A good starting point is to position the mouth of the lower person even with the forehead of the higher person.

Although they can be posed in parallel position (both subjects facing the same direction), a more interesting dynamic can be achieved by having them pose at 45-degree angles to each other, so their shoulders face in toward one another. With this pose you can create a number of variations by moving them closer or farther apart.

Another intimate pose is to have two profiles facing each other. One should still be higher than the other, as this allows you to create an implied

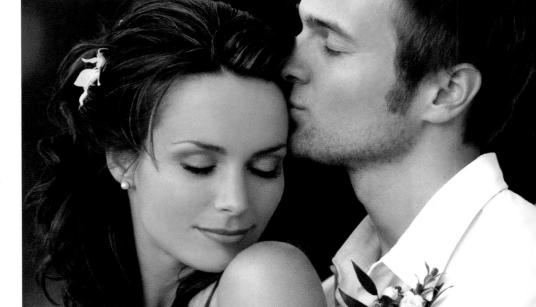

Gordon Nash created this lovely portrait of bride and groom that adorns the opening page of his website. He shot the image with a Nikon D2H and 135mm f/2.0 lens wide open at ISO 640. The pose is elegant: the bride turns back toward the groom, head tipped toward the near shoulder in the classical feminine pose. The sheer bliss of the emotion captured is amazing. Gordon had them close their eyes, which helped convey the emotion.

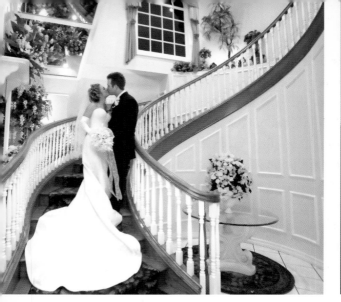

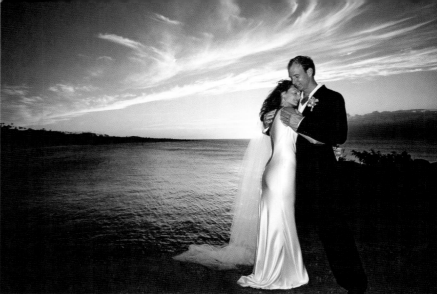

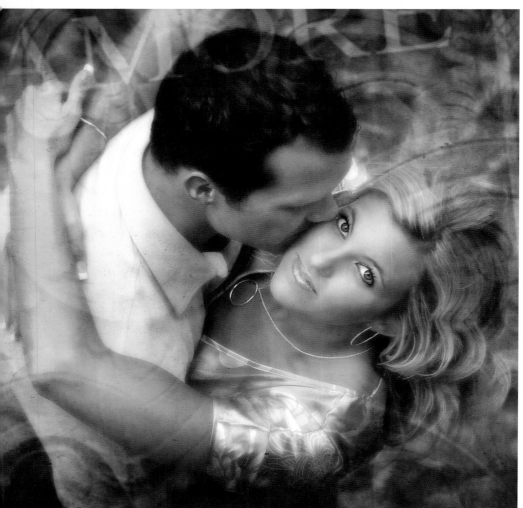

TOP LEFT—Here, a spiral staircase serves as the setting for a formal portrait of the bride and groom kissing. Once a prime location like this is found, it can be used for most if not all of the formal pictures. Photograph by Ben Chen. **TOP RIGHT**—This wide-angle portrait captures the emotion and beauty of a Hawaiian wedding. Gordon Nash shot into the setting sun and popped a straight flash on his couple, an effect that brought out the striking beauty of the dress. The pose is simple: embrace and lean into each other. **LEFT**—An interesting vantage point is from above the couple. Notice that diagonal lines abound in this square composition. On separate layers, the word "Amore" and various textures were incorporated into this image and erased from the faces. Photograph by JB Sallee.

diagonal line between their eyes, which also gives the portrait direction. Since this type of image is fairly close up, make sure that the frontal planes of the subjects' faces are roughly parallel so that you can hold the focus on both.

The formal portraits of the bride and groom together are significant images that demand special time and an understanding of formal posing and lighting techniques. Often the photographer will arrange to make the formal portraits on the day of the wedding, but several hours before the day's schedule commences. Couples relish the alone time and (in addition to an engagement session; see page 86) it is a good opportunity for the photographer to break the ice with the couple.

28. Adding a Third Person

A group portrait of three is still small and intimate. It lends itself well to a pyramid- or diamond-shaped composition, or an inverted triangle, all of which are pleasing to the eye. Don't simply adjust the height of the faces so that each is at a different level; turn the shoulders of those at either end of the group in toward the central person as a means of looping the group together. You can also try creating a diagonal line with the faces at different heights and all the people in the group touching. Or, create a bird's-eye view—cluster the group together, grab a stepladder or other high vantage point, and you've got a lovely arrangement. It's what photographer Norman Phillips calls "a bouquet." For a simple variation, have the people turn their backs to each other, so they are all facing out of the triangle.

TRY CREATING A DIAGONAL LINE WITH THE FACES AT DIFFERENT HEIGHTS AND ALL THE PEOPLE IN THE GROUP TOUCHING.

29. Adding a Fourth and Fifth Person

As you photograph more group portraits, you will find that even numbers of people are harder to pose than odd. Three, five, seven, or nine people seem much easier to photograph than similarly sized groups of an even number. The reason is that the eye and brain tend to accept the disorder of odd-numbered objects more readily than even-numbered objects. (*Note:* As you add more people to a group, remember to do everything you can to keep the film plane parallel to the plane of the group's faces in order to ensure that everyone is sharply focused.)

With four people, you can simply add a person to the existing poses of three described above—with the following advice in mind. First, be sure to keep the eye height of the fourth person different from any of the others in the group. Second, be aware that the faces will now begin forming shapes within your composition. Think in terms of pyramids, extended triangles,

Seated Men in Groups

Whenever a man is seated it's a good idea to check his clothes. He should have his jacket unbuttoned to prevent it from looking tight. If wearing a tux with tails, he should also avoid sitting on them, as this will alter the shape of the coat. If he has shirt cuffs, they should be pulled down to be visible. And if sitting cross-legged, make sure his socks are pulled up high enough so that you don't see any bare leg.

diamonds, and curved lines. Finally, be aware of lines, shapes, and direction as you build your groups.

An excellent pose for four people is a sweeping curve of three people with the fourth person added below and between the first and second person in the group. Alternately, the fourth person can be positioned slightly outside the group for accent, without necessarily disrupting the harmony of the rest of the group.

30. Photographing Larger Groups

As people gather for large group portraits, have them put their drinks down before they enter the staging area, then arrange the group so that the bride and groom are the center of interest and everyone else's face can be seen (tell everyone that they need to be able to see you with both eyes to be seen in the photo). Look for a high vantage point, such as a balcony or sec-

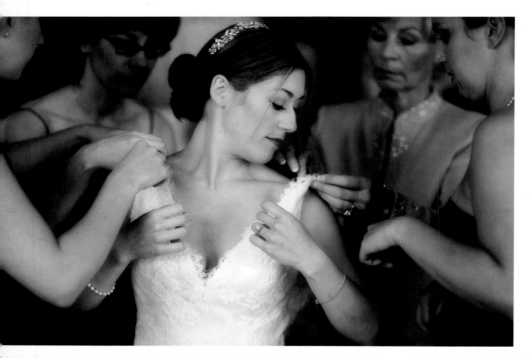

LEFT—Tom Muñoz is not only an expert at choreographing and formally posing events, he is also an expert at pulling the priceless moments out of such scenes. In printing, he darkened the bride's helpers so as to make the bride more dominant in the composition. **BOTTOM LEFT**—The best group photographs are often those made when the people in the group are unaware of the photographer's presence. Here the group is totally absorbed and enjoying what they are seeing. Marc Wesiberg simply adjusted his vantage point to get all of the majority of faces visible. **BOTTOM RIGHT**—Ken Sklute is a master at posing groups. Here, the bride and bridesmaids are lit by available light from the patio doors. Two armchairs attractively seat four girls, while three stand behind in a highly symmetrical but pleasing composition. Note how the girls seated in the armchairs are forward on the edge of the cushion.

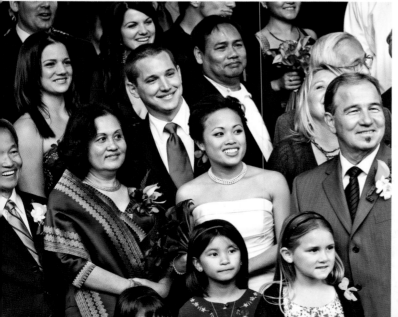

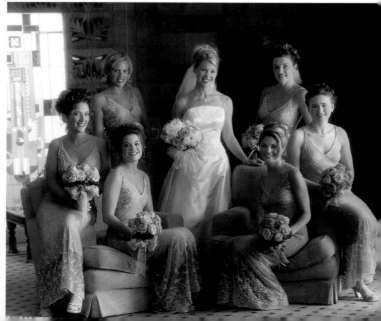

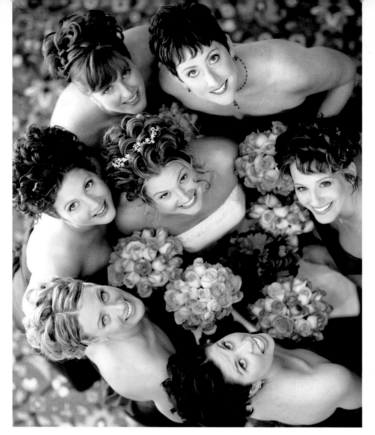

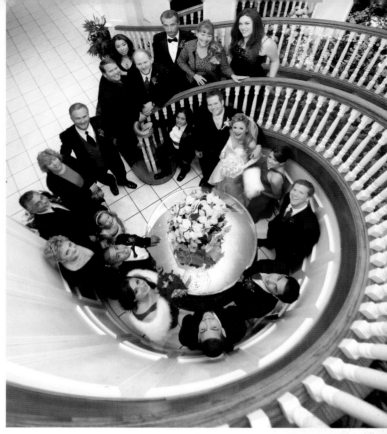

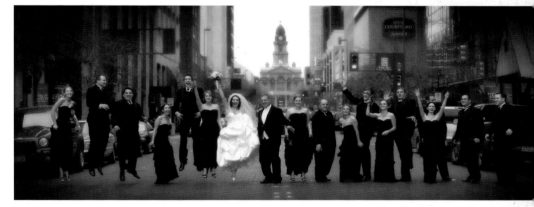

TOP LEFT—This is the "bouquet of flowers" treatment for groups. Shooting from directly above to capitalize on the symmetry of the composition, Dan Doke created a beautiful portrait of the bride and her maids. Using an 85mm lens, the perspective is good and normal. With a wide-angle lens, faces this close to the frame edges would have been distorted. **TOP RIGHT**—Ben Chen used a beautiful spiral staircase as the framework for this formal wedding portrait. He lit the scene with his on-camera 580EX strobe bounced into the ceiling. Notice how each person in the group looks great—even the little ones. **RIGHT**—This is a fun group shot of a huge wedding party done by JB Sallee. Titled *Jump, Damn It!*, this is a very a straight-line composition. The group has a good dynamic created by the fact that over half of the group could not take directions very well. The up-and-down head heights produces its own kind of dynamic line that seems to work in this composition.

ond-story window, from which you can make the portrait. You can also use your trusty stepladder, but be sure someone holds it steady—particularly if you're at the very top. Use a wide-angle lens and focus about a third of the way into the group, using a moderate taking aperture to keep everyone sharply focused. Another trick is to have the last row in a group lean in while having the first row lean back, thus creating a shallower subject plane, making it easier to hold the focus across the entire group.

31. SPEEDING UP YOUR GROUP PORTRAITS

The best man and ushers can usually be persuaded to help organize large group photos. Be sure to have everyone make it sound like fun—it should be. One solution is to make your formal groups at the church door as the couple and bridal party emerge. Everyone in the wedding party is present and the parents are nearby. If you don't have a lot of time to make these groups, this is a great way to get them all at once—in under five minutes.

32. CONTROL THE FOCUS FIELD

Adjust the Camera Angle. With large groups, raising the camera height and angling the camera downward keeps the film plane more parallel to the plane of the group's faces. Doing this does not change the depth of field, but it optimizes the plane of focus to accommodate the depth of the group. This makes it possible to get both the front and back rows in focus.

A SPECIAL GROUP WEDDING PHOTOGRAPH

Marc Weisberg is a perfectionist, but when you see images like this, you know why. "It was late in the day and we were losing sun," he recalls. "The shadows are actually from my trusty Quantum flash, mounted with a quick-release plate on a Bogen tripod at camera left. Instead of using a light meter, which I use now for my large-group portraits, I used my more expensive light meter: my Canon 1-D set to manual. I dialed in the exposure while looking [at the meter scale] through the viewfinder. I shot a Canon "Polaroid" to make sure that my histogram was not clipping the shadows or highlights. Then I set my Quantum flash one stop under and metered the flash output with my Sekonic L508 light meter. Pocket Wizards were used to trigger my Quantum flash." After the shoot, Weisberg added a few enhancements. "The saturation was selectively bumped up with the saturation tool in Photoshop," he says. "The LucisArt filter was also used. Since this filter wreaks havoc on the skin, a mask was created so that I could selectively apply the effects to the dress, bringing out the delicate folds, and to the shoes and tuxedos, to bring out the highlights better. I also used the LucisArt filter with a mask to bring out texture details in the walls, terra cotta tiles, and plants."

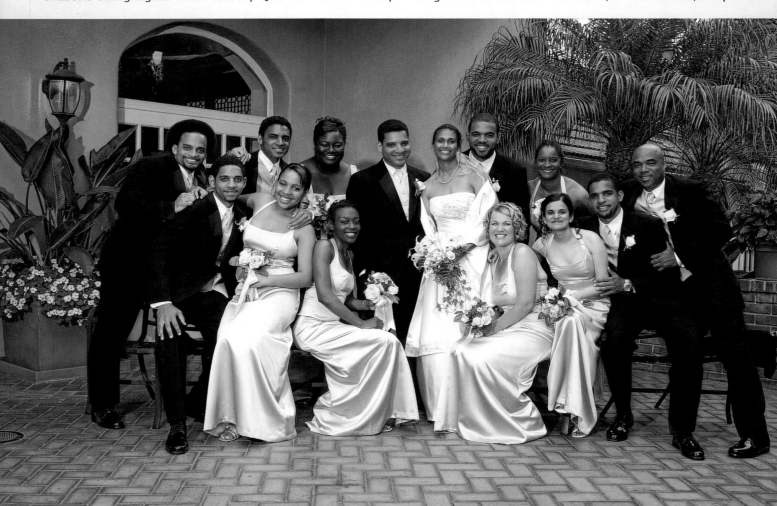

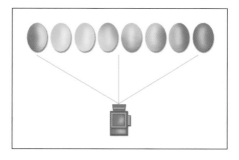

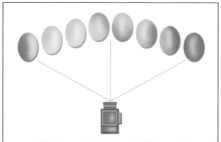

When photographing a group in a straight line, those closest to the center of the line are closest to the lens. Those on the ends of the line are farther away from the lens. When you "bend" the group, you can make each person the same distance from the lens, thus requiring the same amount of depth of field to render them sharply. Diagram concept by Norman Phillips; diagram by Shell Dominica Nigro.

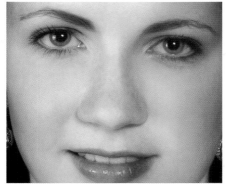

Nick Adams made this beautiful bridal portrait using a 4x3-foot softbox as a main light and two monolights behind a 6x8 foot scrim for fill. The main and fill lights were about equal intensity on either side of the camera. Reflectors were also used at either side of the bride to help redirect stray light. A monolight with beauty dish was added high above the bride and angled down to create an elegant hair light. You can see in the closeup image that the light above the camera is creating a very subtle shadow under her nose. You can also see the positions of the lights by analyzing the catchlights in the bride's eyes.

Adjust the Subject Distance. If your subjects are in a straight line, those at the ends of the group will be proportionately farther away from the lens than those in the middle of the lineup (unless you are working at a great distance from the subjects). As a result, those farthest from the lens will be difficult to keep in focus. The solution is to bend the group, having the middle of the group step back and the ends of the group step forward so that all of the people are at the same relative distance to the camera. To the camera, the group will still look like a straight line, but by distorting the plane of sharpness you will be able to accommodate the entire group.

33. REFINE THE MAIN AND FILL LIGHTS

Because of the hurried nature of the wedding day, it is sometimes impossible to give the lighting the same degree of complexity you would for a studio shoot. However, with an assistant, and a little bit of time you can pull off some beautifully lit formal portraits the day of the wedding. The key to doing this, is understanding the concepts of studio lighting. The two lighting sources that will have the biggest impact are the main and fill lights.

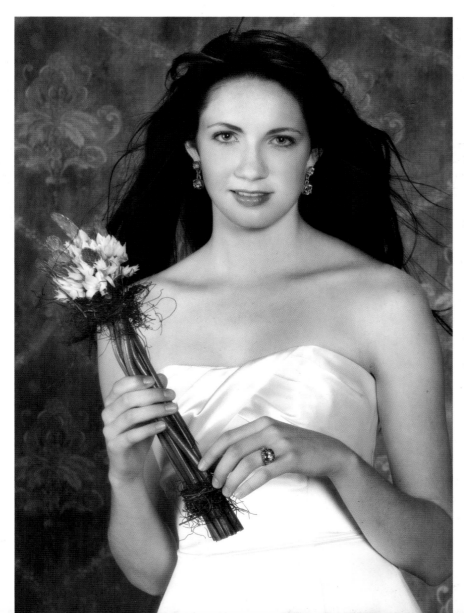

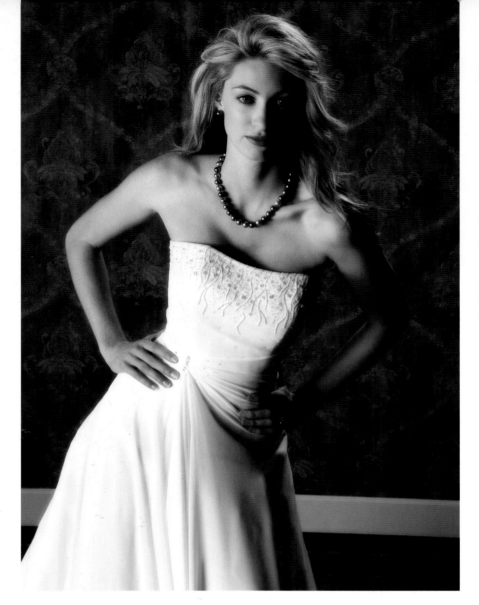

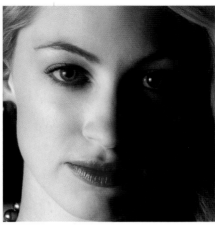

For this formal portrait, Nick Adams used a softbox at head height and to the left of the camera at almost 90 degrees. He used no fill light but did use a dramatic hair light to accent the bride's lovely hair. You can see the position of the main light in the closeup image.

The main light is the light source that creates the visible pattern of light and shadow on the subject's face. For this, most photographers opt to use a diffused source. This could be window light diffused through sheer curtains, soft sky light at the edge of a shady area, or strobe light diffused by an umbrella or softbox.

The fill light is used to lighten the shadows created by the main light. To do this, the fill light should be at least a little weaker than the main light (so it does not create a second set of shadows). Fill light may be created using a reflector or by adding a small diffused light close to the camera.

FILL LIGHT MAY BE CREATED USING A REFLECTOR OR BY ADDING A SMALL DIFFUSED LIGHT CLOSE TO THE CAMERA.

34. CONTROL THE HAIR LIGHT

The hair light is an optional light that can be used to accent the subject's hair and create highlights that help separate it from the background. Adding barn doors to this light (black, metallic, adjustable flaps that can be opened or closed to control the width of the beam of the light) will help keep the light just where you want it and prevent stray light from hitting the camera lens, reducing the potential for lens flare. Hair lights are frequently undiffused sources, so they are normally adjusted to a reduced power setting. In some cases, however, strip lights (small softboxes) are used as hair lights because of their easy mobility and broad diffused highlights.

35. USE A BACKGROUND LIGHT

The background light is a low-output light. It is used to illuminate the background so that the subject and background will separate tonally. The background light is usually used on a stand placed directly behind the subject,

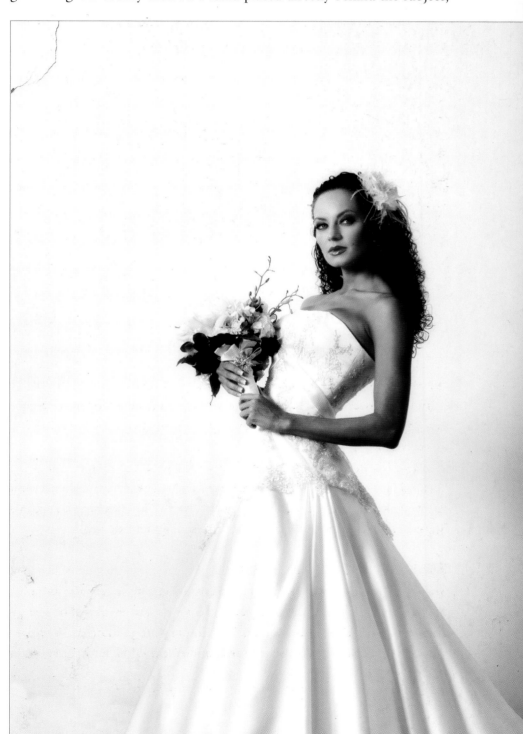

Here is a good example of a short lighting, where the main light is illuminating the side of the face turned away from the camera, so that the shadow side of the face is revealed to the lens. Nick Adams used a single softbox as the main light. The white dress and wall provided ample fill, so no fill source needed to be added.

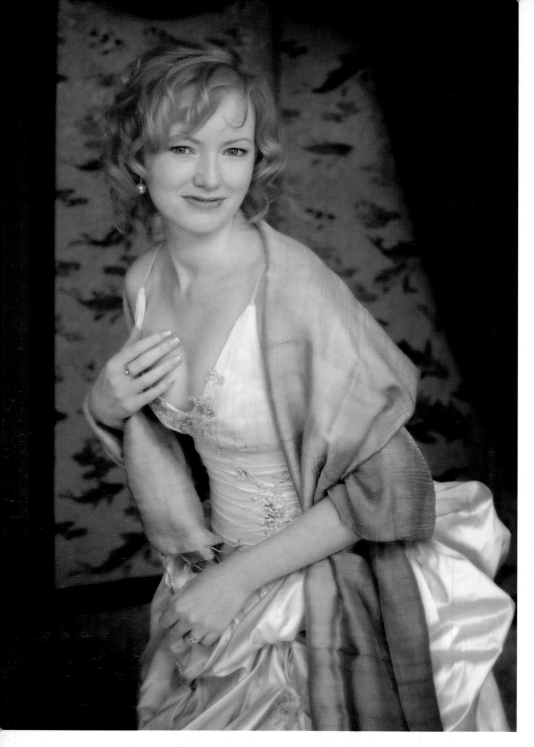

David Williams created this wonderful bridal portrait in his studio, using daylight streaming in through two French doors and a silver reflector thrown onto the floor to kick light up into the folds of the wedding dress. The image was made with a Fuji Finepix S5 Pro with a Sigma EX DC 18–50mm f/2.8 macro lens. Aside from cropping to straighten the verticals, this image is straight from camera.

THESE ADD HIGHLIGHTS TO THE SIDES OF THE FACE OR BODY TO INCREASE THE FEELING OF DEPTH AND RICHNESS IN A PORTRAIT.

out of view of the camera lens. It can also be placed on a higher stand or boom and directed onto the background from either side of the set.

36. ADD KICKER LIGHTS

Kickers are optional lights that are used in much the same way as hair lights. These add highlights to the sides of the face or body to increase the feeling of depth and richness in a portrait. Because they are used behind the subject, they produce highlights with great brilliance, as the light just glances off the skin or clothing. Since kickers are set behind the subject, barn doors should be used to control the light.

37. Choose Broad or Short Lighting

There are two basic types of portrait lighting. Broad lighting means that the main light is illuminating the side of the face turned toward the camera (the more visible side of the face). This is used less frequently than short lighting because it flattens and de-emphasizes facial contours. It is often used, however, to widen a very thin or long face.

Short lighting means that the main light is illuminating the side of the face turned away from the camera (the less visible side of the face). Short lighting emphasizes facial contours and can be used as a corrective lighting technique to narrow a round or wide face. When used with a weak fill light, short lighting produces a dramatic look with bold highlights and pronounced shadows.

38. Lighting Tips from Mauricio Donelli

According to Mauricio Donelli, "The most important thing when creating a spectacular and beautiful image of a bride is to be very, very fast. Own the situation and give the bride the confidence to be her most beautiful in front of your lens. The essence of this philosophy is to take the pictures quickly—if you lose control and spend too much time evaluating the moment, you

With a single strobe in a round softbox positioned close to the bride and groom (on a light stand or held by an assistant), you can create diverse, wonderful images in a very quick time. Photographs by Mauricio Donelli.

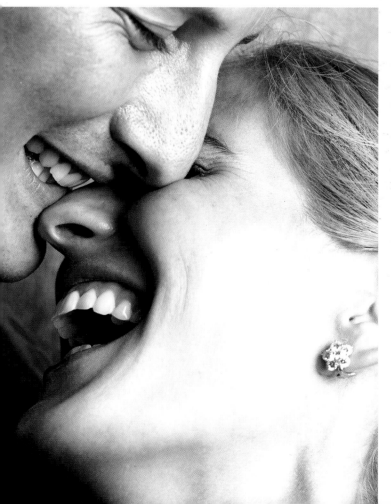

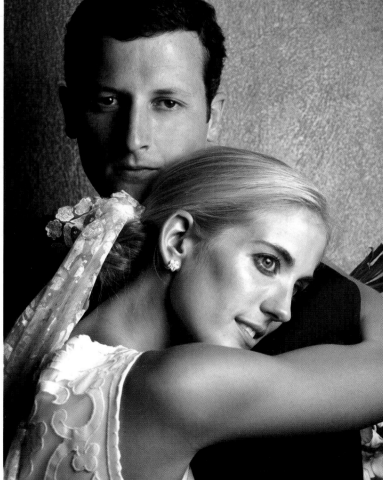

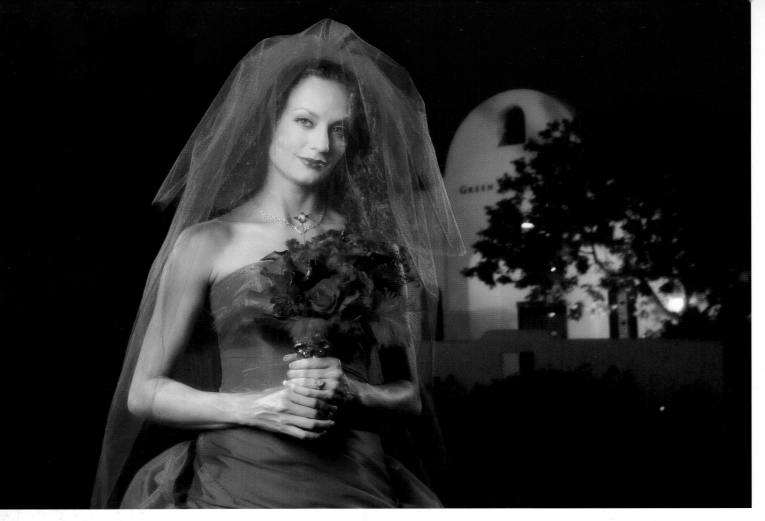

will freeze everything and lose the perfect image." To do this, Donelli uses the D2X and the Leaf back 28 for the Mamiya.

"I don't work with too much artificial light," he also notes. "Also, if most of the situations are being taken at night, the fact is that I work a lot with very slow shutter speeds. This gives a good mix between the flash and the ambient light presence. Also, you can work with the single bulbs that you find in ceilings and walls and place them behind the subject to give an effect of warmth and depth. Sometimes we don't need to use a lot of light. Much of the time, my pictures are taken with natural light and filled with mobile flash from the camera. I prefer the Metz 60-CT4 series. They are the best I've used for this type of fill."

"It is important to have a good, lightweight tripod with you, as well as one or two assistants working around the subject with flashes. Of course, you will need to trigger them from the camera with radio-controlled slaves. They work effectively and are very handy to use with the flash on a monopod. Also, it is important to have a decent-size reflectors (LiteDiscs) to reflect light back onto your subject's shadow areas."

As for power, Donelli says that he never uses generators, because his weddings almost always take place in hotels or homes. "When they do the

This stunning night portrait by Nick Adams illustrates Rembrandt lighting (note the diamond-shaped highlight on the shadow side of the face) and broad lighting. Adams used a softbox for the main light and a hair light to illuminate the bride's hair and veil. Notice the difference in intensity between the main light and the hair light. In order to record background detail at night, Nick slowed the shutter speed to $3/10$ second. The taking aperture was f/7.1.

weddings in open areas and put up tents," he notes, "they need to have light too, so I always ask the wedding coordinators to provide two or three plugs for my monolight-mounted round softbox inside the tent. I never use more than one, but I travel with two in case one goes bad."

39. LOOK FOR THE CLASSIC LIGHTING PATTERNS

While the classic lighting patterns do not have to be used with absolute precision, it is essential to know what they are and how to achieve them. If, for instance, you are photographing your bride and groom outdoors, you can position a single main light to produce the desired lighting pattern and ratio, and use the ambient light (shade, or sun as backlighting) as the fill light. No other lights are needed to produce any of the five basic portrait setups. Use of reflectors, instead of an independent fill light or kickers, may accomplish much the same results in terms of controlling light. Basically, however, each of the lighting patterns takes its personality from the placement of the main light, so this is the most important source to consider.

LEFT—Cherie Steinberg Coté photographed this unusual bridal gown, veil, and hat. Because of the size of the hat, the softbox was lowered to a little below face height, producing a hybrid split lighting. The close proximity and softness of the light causes the light to wrap around the contours of the bride's face, with no shadow edges. **RIGHT**—This beautiful image was made with a single softbox and a silver reflector feathered for minimal fill. The lighting is true Rembrandt style with a perfect triangular highlight on the shadow side of her face. Note, too, the elegant posing of the hands. Photograph by Cherie Steinberg Coté.

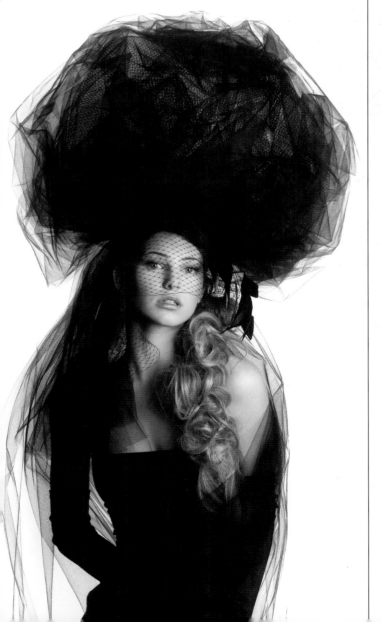

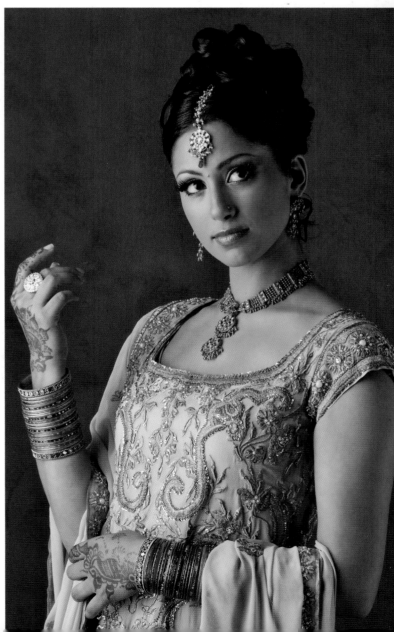

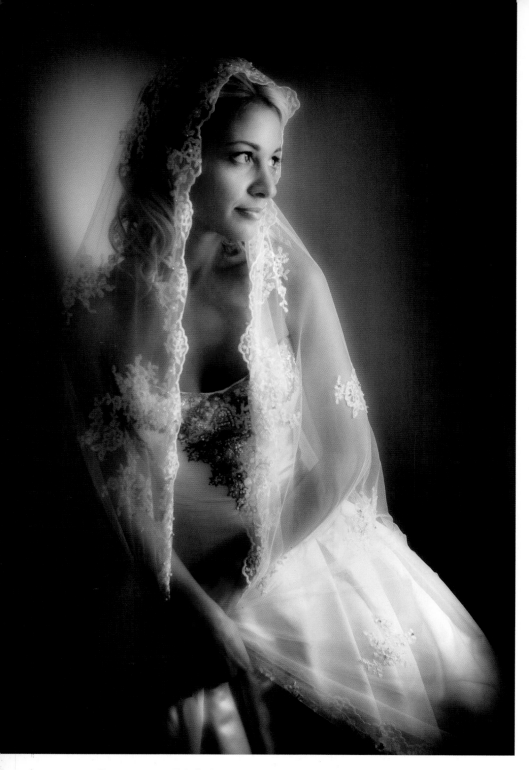

The position of the main light and the turn of the head dictates the type of lighting pattern that will be produced. In this exceptional image by Dan Doke, the bride was lit with a modified profile-lighting pattern. Her head was not fully turned in the traditional profile pose, and as a result the main light is not a true backlight (although it is behind the bride).

Paramount Lighting. In Paramount lighting, sometimes called butterfly lighting or glamour lighting, the main light is placed high and directly in front of the face. This gives a symmetrical, butterfly-shaped shadow directly beneath the subject's nose; it also tends to emphasize cheekbones and good skin. The fill light is placed at the subject's head height directly under the main light. Since both the main and fill lights are on the same side of the camera, a reflector is used on the opposite of the subject to fill in the

THE FILL LIGHT IS PLACED AT THE SUBJECT'S HEAD HEIGHT DIRECTLY UNDER THE MAIN LIGHT.

deep shadows on the neck and shaded cheek. The hair light is used opposite the main light and placed so that it does not skim onto the face of the subject. The background light (if used) should be low and behind the subject, forming a semi-circle of illumination background.

Loop Lighting. Loop lighting is a minor variation of Paramount lighting and is ideal for people with average, oval-shaped faces. The main light is lowered and moved more to the side of the subject so that the shadow under the nose becomes a small loop on the shadow side of the face. The fill light is placed on the opposite side of the camera from the main light, close to the camera lens. (*Note:* Be sure to evaluate this from the camera position, making sure the fill light does not cast a shadow of its own.) In loop lighting, the hair light and background lights are used the same way they are in Paramount lighting.

Rembrandt Lighting. Rembrandt lighting, also called 45-degree lighting, is characterized by a small, triangular highlight on the shadowed

LOOP LIGHTING IS A VARIATION OF PARAMOUNT LIGHTING AND IS IDEAL FOR PEOPLE WITH AVERAGE, OVAL-SHAPED FACES.

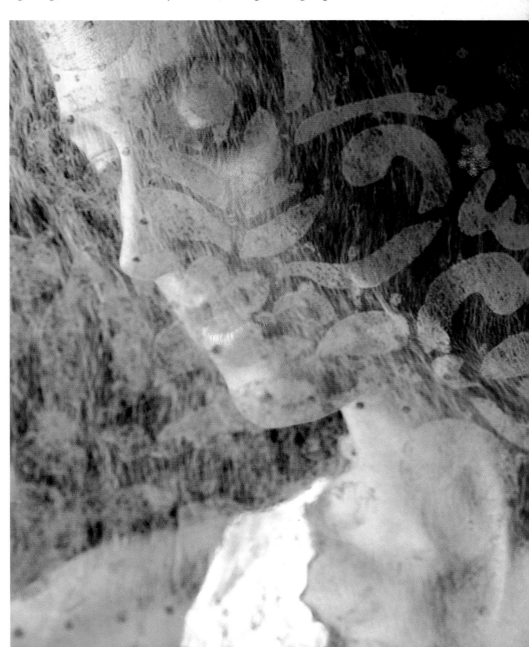

Here, Mauricio Donelli used a softbox to create rim lighting. By feathering the light (using only the edge of the light on the subject) he created a row of specular highlights along the bridge of the nose and on the bride's forehead. The veil softens the entire image and only the specular highlights define its sharpness.

FIND THE DIRECTION

Even experienced photographers sometimes can't tell the direction of the light in open shade, particularly midmorning or midafternoon. A simple trick is to use a piece of gray or white folded card—an index card works well. Crease the card in the middle to form an open V shape. Hold the card vertically with the point of the V pointed toward the camera, then compare the two sides of the V. The card will tell you if the light is coming from the right or left and how intense the ratio between highlight and shadow is. Held with the fold horizontal and pointed toward the camera, the card will tell you if the light is vertical in nature, coming from above. Using this handy tool, you can often gauge when a slight adjustment in subject or camera position will salvage an otherwise unusable setting.

cheek of the subject. This is created by moving the main light lower and farther to the side than in loop and Paramount lighting; the main light comes almost from the subject's side, depending on how far his or her head is turned away from the camera. The fill light is used in the same manner as it is for loop lighting, although a weaker setting is often used to accentuate the shadow-side highlight. The hair light is often used a little closer to the subject for more brilliant highlights in the hair. The background light is in the standard position. With this setup, kickers are often used to delineate the sides of the face. (*Note:* To ensure they are not shining directly into the lens, place your hand between the subject and the camera on the axis of the kicker. If your hand casts a shadow on the lens, then the kicker is shining directly into the lens and should be adjusted.)

Split Lighting. Split lighting occurs when the main light illuminates only half the face. This is produced by placing the main light low and to the side of the subject. Depending on how far the subject is turned from the camera, the main light may even be slightly behind the subject. This placement of the main light creates a nice slimming effect. It can also be used with a weak fill to hide facial irregularities. For a dramatic effect, use split lighting with no fill light. The fill light, hair light, and background light are used normally for split lighting.

Profile or Rim Lighting. Profile or rim lighting is used when the subject's head is turned 90 degrees away from the camera lens. It is a dramatic style of lighting used to accent elegant features. It is used less frequently now than in the past, but it remains a stylish type of portrait lighting.

To light the profile, the main light is placed behind the subject so that it illuminates the far side of the face and leaves a polished highlight along its outline. Care should be taken so that the light principally accents the face, rather than the hair or neck. In this setup, the fill light is moved to the same side of the camera as the main light and a reflector is used to fill in the shadows. An optional hair light can be used on the opposite side of the main light for better tonal separation of the hair from the background. The background light is used normally.

DEPENDING ON HOW FAR THE SUBJECT IS TURNED FROM THE CAMERA, THE MAIN LIGHT MAY EVEN BE SLIGHTLY BEHIND THE SUBJECT.

You can even create an elegant profile of the bride with a single flash used as a backlight, outlining the edges of her face, neck, and the wedding veil. With the daylight as fill, only one light is required to produce an elegant, classically lit portrait.

40. Avoid Double Shadows and Double Catchlights

Adding a fill light can pose two problems. If placed too close to the subject or is too intense, the fill light will produce its own set of specular highlights that show up in the shadow area of the face, making the skin appear excessively oily. To solve the problem, move the camera and light back slightly or move the fill light laterally away from the camera. In many cases, the fill light also creates a second set of catchlights in the subject's eyes. This gives the subject a directionless gaze, so these catchlights are usually removed in postproduction. When using a large diffused fill light, there is usually not a problem with dual catchlights. Instead, the fill produces a large, milky highlight that is much less objectionable.

41. Understand Lighting Ratios

The term "lighting ratio" describes the difference in intensity between the shadow and highlight side of the face. It is expressed numerically: 2:1, 3:1, etc. In the studio, one can control the ratio precisely; in the field, your goal should be more general. Is there detail in both important highlight and shadow areas? Are the shadow areas too dark and lifeless?

With digital, one can inspect the lighting by firing a few test frames. (This is particularly important when using flash, since you cannot see lighting effect with the naked eye.) Professionals should also carry an incident flash meter, which also measures ambient light. From the subject position, you can then measure the highlight side of the face separately from the shadow side of the face, thus determining the difference between the two and thus the effective lighting ratio.

In a 2:1 lighting ratio, the main and fill light sources are the same intensity. A 3:1 lighting ratio is produced when the main light is one stop greater in intensity than the fill light. In a 4:1 ratio, the main light is 1½ stops greater in intensity than the fill light. In a 5:1 ratio, the main light is two stops greater than the fill light.

42. Avoid Overlighting

In setting the lights, it is important that you position them gradually, studying the effect as you aim each additional source at the subject. If you merely point the light directly at the subject, you will probably overlight the person, producing pasty highlights with no detail. Instead, feather the light so

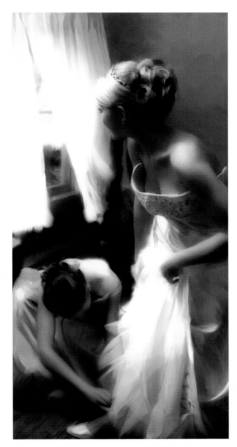

Window light is not the main light here, although you can see its effect. A softbox, positioned above and to camera left, actually created the highlights in the bride's hair and on her shoulder. Bruce Dorn, a cinematographer in his previous career, is used to augmenting natural light with other lights and balancing their output. Bruce also added a few brush-stroke effects in Corel Painter.

that you employ the edge of the light to illuminate the subject. This will add brilliance to your highlights, enhancing the illusion of depth. (*Note:* Sometimes feathering won't produce the desired highlight brilliance. If this happens, making a lateral adjustment to the light or moving it back from its current position will usually rectify the situation.)

43. EVALUATE YOUR OPTIONS

Weddings involve almost every kind of light you can imagine—open shade, bright sun, dusk, dim room light, and every combination in between. Savvy wedding photographers must feel at home in all these different situations and know how to get great pictures in them.

For example, imagine a courtyard where the main light is diffused daylight coming in through an archway. Here, the ambient fill level would be very low; there may be no auxiliary light sources nearby. Unless your goal was to produce high-contrast lighting (not great for brides), you would need to raise the level of the ambient or fill light. You might add light locally (i.e., on the subject via a silver reflector). This is a quick solution that could be ideal if you are pressed for time or only need to make a couple of shots in the area. Alternately, you might add some fill universally, raising the overall interior light level by using ceiling-bounce strobes. This solution involves more setup time and effort, but it could allow you to shoot in a number of locations within the location, not just the one closest to the archway.

Learning to control, predict and alter whatever type of lighting encountered will allow the photographer to create great wedding pictures all day and all night long.

44. FIND AND USE OPEN SHADE

Open shade is soft light that is reflected from the sky on overcast days. It is different than shade created by direct sunlight being blocked by obstructions, such as trees or buildings. Open shade can be particularly harsh, especially at midday when the sun is directly overhead. In this situation, open shade takes on the same characteristics as overhead sunlight, creating deep shadows in the eye sockets and under the noses and chins of the subjects.

Open shade can, however, be tamed and made useful by finding an overhang, like tree branches or a porch, which blocks the overhead light but allows soft shade light to filter in from the sides, producing direction and contouring

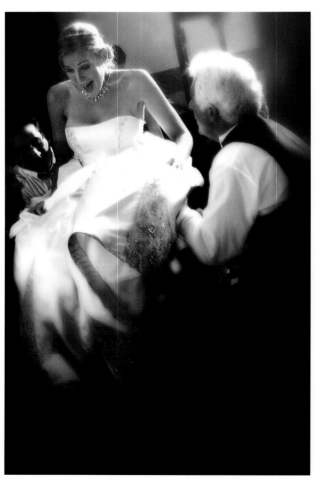

A strong backlight rim lit the bride and the gentlemen hoisting her chair. Bruce Dorn used the light to best advantage and increased his exposure level to capture the shadow side of the event. This blew out the highlights, but the shot is still a huge success because of its spontaneity. It's a good example of reacting quickly to what light you have to work with. In Photoshop, Dorn also softened the background to make it look almost misty.

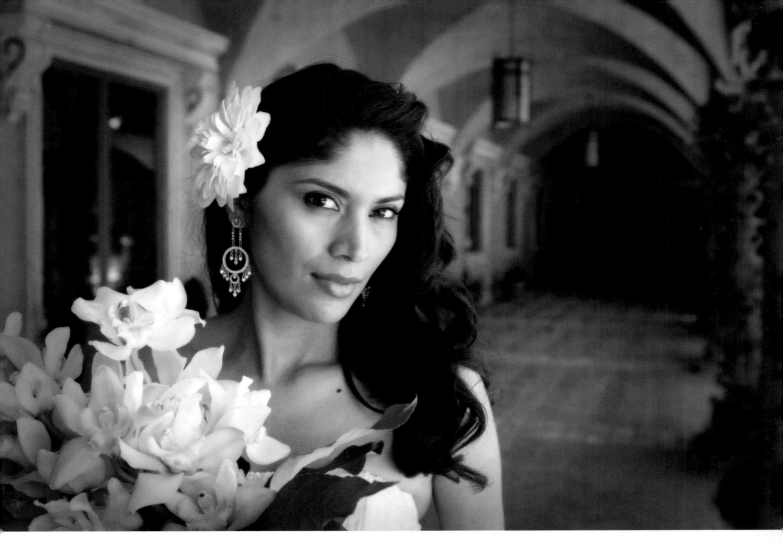

Ken Sklute often takes advantage of portico lighting, places where the daylight is blocked from overhead but filters in from the side for beautiful side lighting of the subject. Here, the adobe walls inside the portico created the right shade of fill light to perfectly compliment a bridal portrait. In Photoshop, Ken added a layer that softened the skin tones slightly and boosted the saturation to bring out the true adobe color.

on the subject. This cancels out the overhead nature of the light and produces excellent modeling on the face.

If forced to shoot your subjects out in unobstructed open shade, you must fill in the shade with a frontal flash or reflector. If shooting the bride or the bride and groom, a reflector held close to and beneath your subjects should suffice for filling in the shadows created by open shade. If photographing more than two people, then fill-flash is called for. The intensity of the light should be about equal to the daylight exposure.

45. WORKING WITH DIRECT SUNLIGHT

When forced to photograph in bright sunlight, begin by turning your subjects so the direct sunlight is backlighting or rim lighting them. This negates the harshness of the light and prevents your subjects from squinting. Then, fill in the backlight with strobe or reflectors (being careful to avoid underexposure). It is best to add $\frac{1}{3}$ to $\frac{1}{2}$ stop exposure in backlit situations portraits in order to "open up" the skin tones.

Images made in bright sunlight are unusually contrasty. To lessen that contrast, try using telephoto lenses or zooms, which have less inherent contrast than shorter, prime lenses. If shooting digitally, you can adjust your contrast preset to a low setting or shoot in RAW mode, where you can fully control image contrast post-capture.

If the sun is low in the sky, you can use cross lighting to get good modeling on your subject. You must be careful, however, to position the subject so that the sun's side lighting does not hollow out their eye socket on

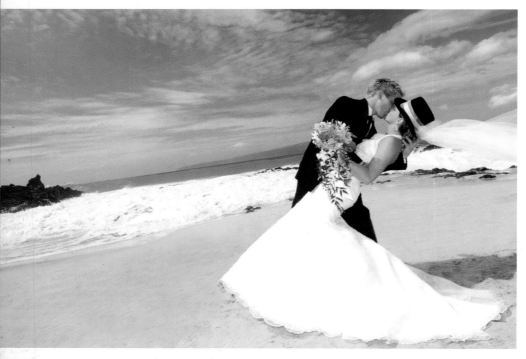

LEFT—Working in mid-day sunlight, Gordon Nash fired a strobe from the camera position. This was slightly less powerful than the daylight, counteracting the directly overhead sunlight. The image was made with a Nikon D200 and 12–24mm f/4.0 lens. **BELOW**—Joe Photo counted on the brilliant contrast of a low sun to make this stunning portrait of a bride. He softened the image extensively in Photoshop and selectively darkened areas that robbed attention from the bride. Joe faced the bride into the sun in order to create a nice lighting pattern on her face from the angle at which he was photographing her.

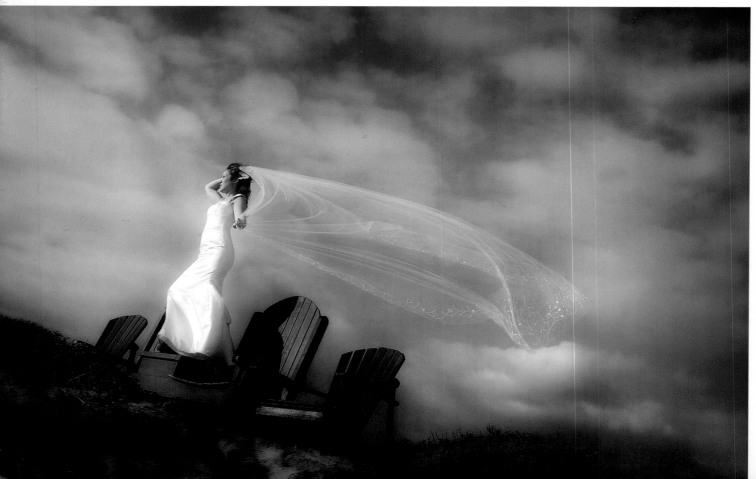

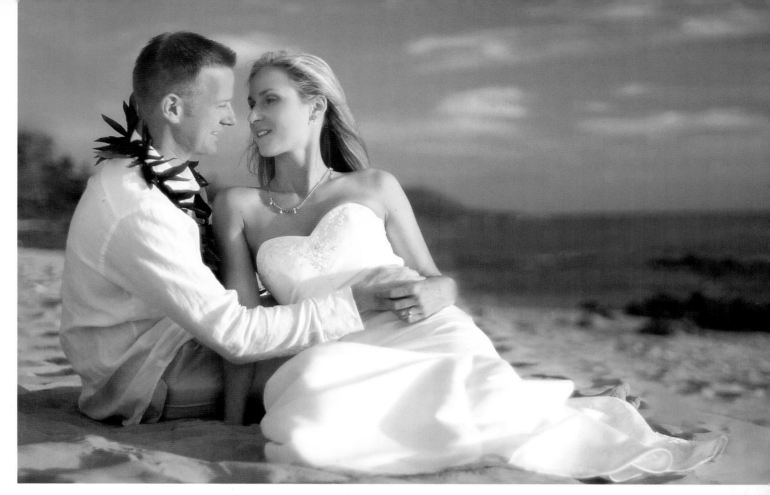

ABOVE—The rays of the setting sun become more diffuse as the sun nears the horizon. Here, Maui wedding specialist Gordon Nash captured a loving portrait in fading sunlight. He used a Nikon D2H and 50mm f/1.4 lens wide open. He exposed in RAW mode and warmed the color temperature to a more golden glow to enhance the light. Notice how the light backlit her and front lit him. No fill was required. **RIGHT**—Direct sunlight streamed in through an overhang (a good illustration of how bad found lighting can be). No fill light was added. Bruce Dorn made the very best of this by biasing his exposure to hold most of the shadow detail, while sacrificing a few of the pure white highlights. Subject positioning was crucial, as he wanted to minimize the highlight areas on the dress. He softened and blurred the background, burned in some of the grass, but did little else.

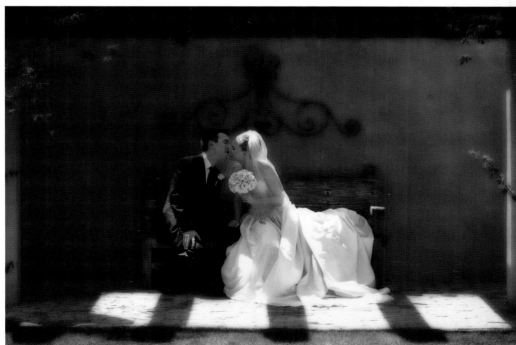

the highlight side. Subtle repositioning will usually correct this. You'll also need to use fill light on the shadow side to preserve detail. Try to keep your fill-flash output about ½ to one stop less than your daylight exposure.

46. WATCH THE ROOM LIGHT

Many hotels use coiled fluorescent bulbs instead of tungsten-filament bulbs in the room lamps. Be on the lookout for them, because these fluorescents will not have the same warming quality as tungsten bulbs and could turn things a bit green. You may have to change your white balance, or use an auto or custom white balance setting, in these situations.

47. TAKE ADVANTAGE OF WINDOW LIGHT

One of the most flattering types of lighting you can use is window lighting. It is soft, minimizes facial imperfections, yet provides a directional source for good facial modeling with low to moderate contrast. Window light is usually a fairly bright light and it is infinitely variable, changing almost by the minute. This allows a great variety of moods, depending on how far you position your subject from the light.

Since daylight falls off rapidly once it enters a window, and is much weaker several feet from the window than it is closer to the window, great care must be taken in determining exposure (particularly when creating group portraits, for which you will usually need to use reflectors to balance the overall light).

LEFT—One of the tricks the wedding photographer employs when shooting by window light is to shoot in RAW mode and warm the color temperature in the RAW file processing. That's what was done with this Gordon Nash portrait, which was made by the light of really large windows to the bride's left. The change in color temperature gives the image a golden, sunlit look. **RIGHT**—A broad expanse of window light from a covered patio to the bride's right created a wall of soft wraparound light that softly defined the contours of her face. Photograph by Joe Buissink.

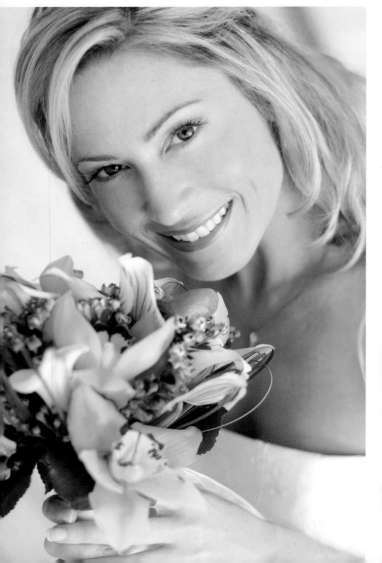

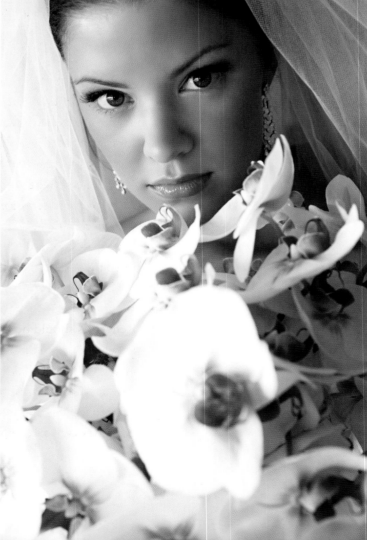

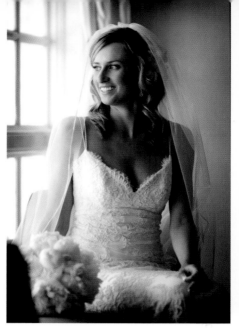

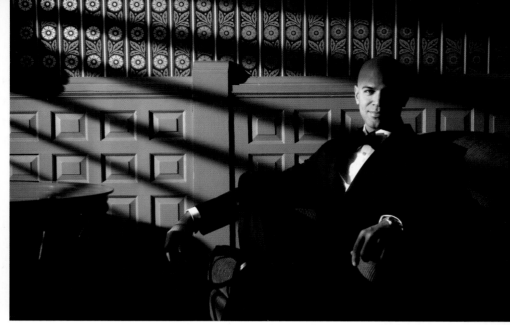

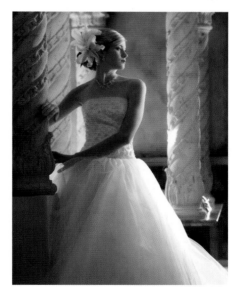

TOP LEFT—This is a very good example of the wraparound nature of window light. In this image by Joe Photo, no fill was used. **TOP RIGHT**—This is an unusual use of window light. Most times photographers look for diffused window light. Cherie Steinberg Coté used direct sunlight, which formed a radial spoke pattern, to light her groom. Careful positioning helped light his face and gobo his forehead and the top of his head for a very fashion-forward image. No fill was used, and Cherie darkened the hands in Photoshop. **LEFT**—Bruce Dorn created this stunning bridal portrait with a Westcott Spiderlite TD5 equipped with five 5500K daylight fluorescent coils in a 36x48-inch softbox. Even though the Spiderlite's fluorescents are on the warm side, Dorn decided to warm the light further by adding a half-CTO gel filter to the softbox. With this light slightly behind the bride, Dorn asked his assistant to position a Westcott Natural Reflector close to the bride to kick in some much-needed light for the overall exposure.

The best quality of window light is found midmorning or midafternoon. Direct sunlight is difficult to work with because of its intensity and the fact that it will often create shadows of the individual windowpanes on the subject. However, you can diffuse overly contrasty window light by taping some acetate diffusion material to the window frame. Light diffused in this manner has the warm feeling of sunlight but without the harsh shadows. (*Note:* If the light is still too harsh, try doubling the thickness of the acetate for more diffusion.) With the light scattered in this way, you may not even need a fill source unless you are working with a larger group. If that is the case, use reflectors to kick light back into the faces of those farthest from the window.

48. REFLECTORS FOR FILL

Reflectors should be fairly large for maximum versatility. Light discs, made of fabric that is mounted on a flexible and collapsible circular frame, come in a variety of diameters and are a very effective means of providing fill-in illumination. They are available from a number of manufacturers and come in silver (for maximum fill output), white, gold foil (for a warming fill light), and black (for blocking light from hitting a portion of the subject). Generally, an assistant is required to position and hold the reflector for maximum effect. Be sure to position reflectors outside the frame and be careful about bouncing light in from beneath your subjects. Lighting coming from under the eye/nose axis is generally unflattering. Try to "focus" your reflectors (this really does require an assistant), so that you are only filling the shadows that need filling in.

49. GETTING THE MOST FROM ON-CAMERA FLASH

On-camera flash should be used sparingly because of the flat, harsh light it produces. As an alternative, many photographers use on-camera flash brackets, which position the flash over and away from the lens, thus minimizing flash red-eye and dropping the harsh shadows behind the subjects—a slightly more flattering light. On-camera flash is often used outdoors, especially with TTL-balanced flash-exposure systems. With such systems, you can adjust the flash output for various fill-in ratios, thus producing consistent exposures. In these situations, the on-camera flash is most frequently used to fill in the shadows caused by the daylight, or to match the ambient light output in order to provide direction to the light.

One of the best means of evaluating flash output and the balance between flash illumination and daylight or room light is by using the camera's LCD screen. While it's not a perfect tool for evaluating subtle exposure effects, it's definitely accurate enough to reveal how well your flash is performing. You can see at a glance if you need to increase or decrease flash output.

ON-CAMERA FLASH SHOULD BE USED SPARINGLY BECAUSE OF THE FLAT, HARSH LIGHT IT PRODUCES.

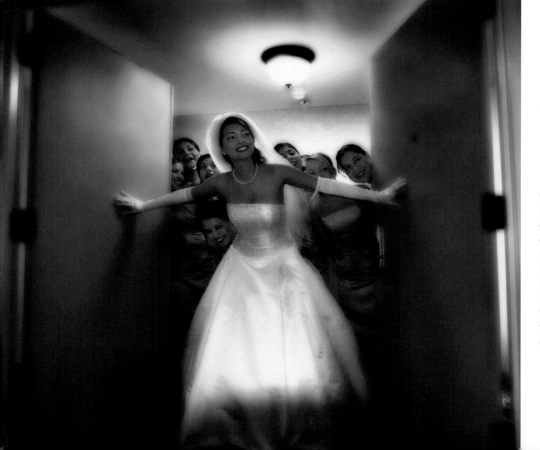

The main light source in this image was an incandescent hall light, which Jerry D let warm the scene by selecting a daylight white-balance setting. He added bounce flash near the camera position to light the bride but he did not overpower the lighting. He actually underexposed the flash a bit to let the room light overpower the flash. He softened the image in Photoshop to produce a dynamic shot of the bride and her attendants.

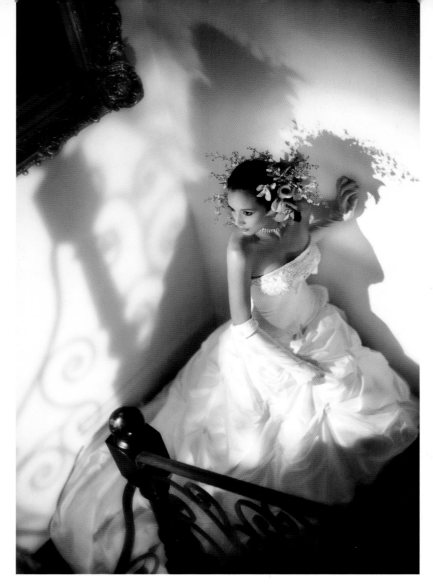

Bruce Dorn combined numerous small light sources as main and accent lights in this beautiful image. Normally, contradictory shadows would be a no-no. Here however, Dorn used them as design elements. You don't see them as confusing, because the lighting is so brilliant.

50. KNOW YOUR FLASH-SYNC SPEED

If using a camera with a focal-plane shutter, you have a flash-sync (or X-sync) setting. When working with flash, employing a shutter speed *faster* than the flash-sync speed will result in images that are only half exposed. You can, however, use any shutter speed *slower* than the flash-sync speed. When you do this, your strobe will fire in synchronization with the shutter, but the shutter will remain open after the flash pop, allowing the ambient light to be recorded. The latest generation of DSLRs use flash-sync shutter speeds up to $\frac{1}{500}$ second, making daylight flash sync at almost any aperture possible. (*Note:* With in-lens blade-type shutters, flash sync occurs at any shutter speed, because there is no focal-plane shutter curtain to cross the film plane.)

51. FLASH OPTIONS

Barebulb. Barebulb flash units are powerful lights that consists of an upright flash tube sealed in a plastic housing for protection. Since there is no reflector, barebulb flash generates light that goes in all directions. It acts more like a large point-source light than a small portable flash.

Light falloff with barebulb is less than with other handheld units, making it ideal for flash-fill situations; you can use as wide a lens as you own and you won't get flash falloff with barebulb flash. Barebulb flash produces a sharp, sparkly light, which is too harsh for almost every type of photography except outdoor fill. The trick is not to overpower the daylight. It is most desirable to let the daylight or twilight backlight your subjects, capitalizing on a colorful sky background if one exists, and use barebulb flash to fill the frontal planes of your subjects.

Barebulb flash units are predominantly manual, meaning you must adjust their intensity by adjusting the flash-to-subject distance or the flash output. Many photographers even mount a sequence of barebulb flash units on light stands at the reception for doing candids on the dance floor.

Diffused Flash. As an alternative to barebulb flash, some photographers like to soften their fill-flash using a softbox. In this situation, it is best to trigger the strobe with a radio remote. This allows you to place the diffused flash at a 30- to 45-degree angle to the subject(s) for dynamic fill-in. For this, it is wise to equal or overpower the daylight exposure slightly so that the off-angle flash acts more like a main light, establishing a lighting pattern. For large group portraits, it may be necessary to use several softboxes (or to use a single one close to the camera) for more even coverage.

52. FLAWLESS FILL-FLASH EXPOSURE

To ensure accurate fill-flash exposures every time, meter the daylight with an incident flashmeter in "ambi" mode. Let's imagine that the metered exposure is $\frac{1}{30}$ second at f/8. Next, meter the flash only. It is desirable for the flash output to be one stop less than the ambient exposure; in this case, you would adjust the flash output or flash distance until your flash reading was f/5.6. You would then set the camera to $\frac{1}{30}$ second at f/8. That's it. You could then set the flash output anywhere from f/8 to f/5.6 and not overpower the daylight; the flash would only fill in the shadows created by the daylight and add sparkle to the eyes.

TTL flash systems are ideal for working in mixed-light situations and are virtually foolproof. They can be balanced with existing light and easily programmed to over- or underpower the available light by simply dialing in flash exposure compensation in $\frac{1}{3}$-stop increments. In TTL flash mode, the flash will react as programmed, cutting or increasing output as you desire in order to optimize the combination of flash and existing light.

53. FLASH FOR THE MAIN LIGHT

When using flash as the main light and ambient light for the fill, it is important to remember that you are balancing two light sources in one scene. The ambient light exposure will control the exposure on both the background and the subjects. The flash exposure will affect only the subjects.

At Twilight. If the light is fading or the sky is brilliant and you want to shoot for optimal color saturation in the background, overpower the daylight with the flash. This is where the flash becomes the main light and the ambient light becomes the fill light. Returning to the situation above, where the daylight exposure was $\frac{1}{30}$ second at f/8, you could adjust your flash output so your flashmeter reading was f/11, one stop more powerful than the daylight. Then, you would set your camera to $\frac{1}{30}$ second at f/11. At these settings, the flash would provide the main light while the soft twilight provided the fill light. This technique works best when the flash is diffused and at an angle to the subjects so there is some discernable lighting pattern. (*Note:* The only problem with this technique is that you will get shadows from the flash. This can be acceptable, however, since there aren't really any shadows coming from the twilight.)

THE AMBIENT LIGHT EXPOSURE WILL CONTROL THE EXPOSURE ON BOTH THE BACKGROUND AND THE SUBJECTS.

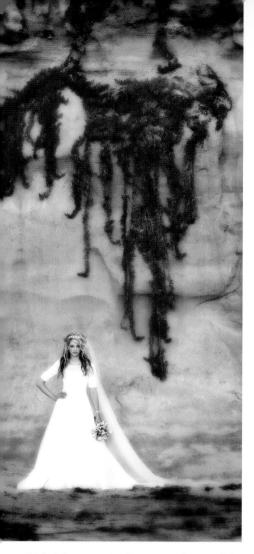

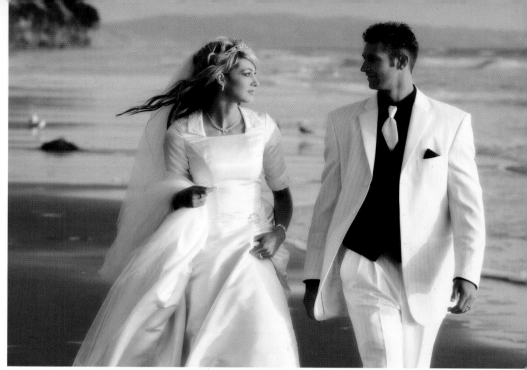

Nick Adams made these two photos eight minutes apart on a beach in California. The vertical image was actually shot in front of a cliff, although it looks like an adobe wall. It was created using natural light with the sun close to the horizon and filtered through the beach's foggy haze. This was behind Nick and to his left. The horizontal image of the same bride with her new husband was shot eight minutes earlier. That little bit of time, according to Nick, made the light in the vertical image cooler and more diffuse. He shot square to the cliff to use it as a backdrop, employing a longer lens (105mm equivalent) to compress the scene. Later, he cranked the contrast way up in Photoshop to produce good separation. He also blurred the piles of seaweed in the foreground and other parts of the image.

On Overcast Days. When the flash exposure and the daylight exposure are identical, the effect is like creating your own sunlight. This technique works particularly well on overcast days when using barebulb flash. Position the flash to the right or left of the subject(s) and raise it up for better modeling. If you want to accentuate the lighting pattern and darken the background and shadows, increase the flash output to ½ to one stop greater than the daylight exposure and expose for the flash exposure. Do not underexpose your background by more than a stop, however, or you will produce an unnatural nighttime effect.

Many times this effect will allow you to shoot out in open shade without fear of creating eye sockets that are hollowed-out by shadow. The overhead nature of the diffused daylight will be overridden by the directional flash, which creates a distinct lighting pattern.

54. ADDING BOUNCE FLASH

Bounce Flash Off Walls and Ceilings. By bouncing the flash off the ceiling, you can achieve soft, directional light that fully illuminates your subjects. When using bounce flash, you must learn to gauge angles and distances. Aim the flash unit at a point on the ceiling that will produce the widest beam of light reflecting back onto your subjects. There are two things to watch out for when using this technique. First, avoid bouncing flash off colored ceilings or walls; you may not be able to compensate for the resulting color cast, even with custom white balance. Second, watch out for excessively overhead lighting. This can be a big problem with high ceilings, producing light that is almost directly overhead in nature—and not the most flattering look for portraits.

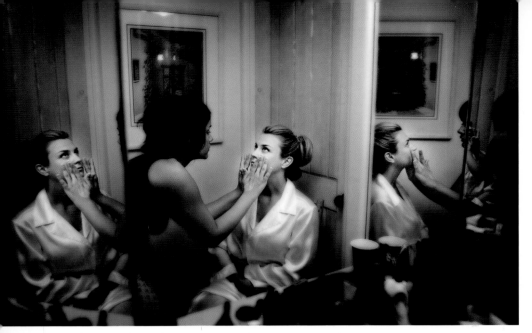

When working with the bride getting ready in dressing rooms, hotel rooms, etc., Joe Photo leaves a bounce flash permanently mounted to his D1X or D2X. The flash has a small reflector that kicks a small percentage of the light forward rather than straight up. The result is a bounce flash with a little direction to it. This image made with 17mm f/2.8 lens used wide open at an exposure of $^1/_{180}$ second at f/2.8.

You don't necessarily have to use your flash-sync speed when making bounce flash exposures. If the room-light exposure is within a stop or two of your bounce-flash exposure ($^1/_{125}$ second at f/4, for example), you can select a slower shutter speed to record more of the ambient room light. If the room light exposure is $^1/_{30}$ second at f/4, for example, expose the bounce-flash photos at $^1/_{30}$ second at f/4 for a balanced flash and room-light exposure. Be wary of shutter speeds longer than $^1/_{15}$ second; the flash will freeze the subject, but the longish shutter speed might produce "ghosting" if your subject is moving. This effect can be quite interesting visually. In fact, many photographers incorporate a slow shutter speed and flash to record a sharp image over a moving one for a painterly effect.

Keep in mind that TTL flash metering systems and auto-flash systems will read bounce-flash situations fairly accurately, but factors such as ceiling distance, color, and absorption qualities can affect proper exposure.

Bounce-Flash Devices. A number of devices on the market are designed to eliminate the excessively overhead quality sometimes found with bounce flash. The Lumiquest ProMax system, for example, mounts on the flash housing and transmits some of the light forward onto the subject, with the remainder of the light being aimed at the ceiling. Lumiquest also offers the Pocket Bouncer, which redirects light at a 90-degree angle from the flash to soften the quality of light and distribute it over a wider area. No exposure compensation is necessary with automatic and TTL flash exposure systems, although operating distances will be somewhat reduced.

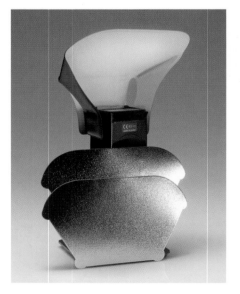

The Lumiquest Bounce Kit (www.lumiquest.com) is a three-piece kit that includes the Pocket Bouncer, gold and silver metallic inserts, and a storage envelope. The Pocket Bouncer redirects light at a 90-degree angle from the flash to soften harsh shadows and more evenly spread the light over a wider area. The gold insert is ideal for late afternoon fill and the silver insert adds a more specular look to the highlights.

55. USING REMOTE TRIGGERING DEVICES

If using multiple flash units (to light the dance floor, for instance), some type of remote triggering device will be needed to sync all the flashes at the instant of exposure. There are a variety of these devices available. Light-actuated slaves are sensitive to the light of a flash unit being fired and fire the flash they are attached to at the same instant they sense a flash going off. Unfortunately, this can be your flash or someone else's—a real drawback to this type of remote flash trigger. Infrared remote flash triggers are more reliable. Since many monolight-type flash units come equipped with an infrared sensor built in, it is a simple matter of syncing the flashes with the appropriate transmitter. A third type, the radio remote triggering device, uses a radio signal that is transmitted when you press the shutter release and then picked up by individual receivers mounted to each flash. These are reliable, but not foolproof; a cordless microphone may trigger them accidentally. Radio remotes transmit signals in either digital or analog form. Digital systems, like the Pocket Wizard, are much more reliable and are not affected by local radio signals. Some photographers will use, as part of the

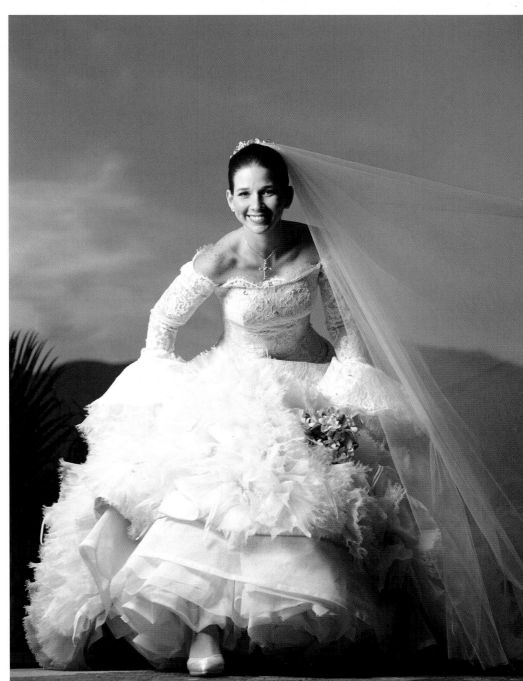

One of the ways to deal with sunlight is to overpower it, as was done here by Mauricio Donelli. He used a closely placed softbox to overpower the daylight reading by about one f-stop so that he could create a defined lighting pattern with the diffused strobe. He takes along at least two battery-powered, self-contained units for such moments as this.

standard equipment, a separate transmitter for as many cameras as are being used (for instance, an assistant's camera), as well as a separate transmitter for the handheld flashmeter, allowing the photographer to take remote flash readings from anywhere in the room.

56. Try the Nikon Speedlight Commander

The latest development in electronic flash is a device Nikon calls the SU-800 Wireless Speedlight Commander that enables you to wirelessly coordinate the independent operation of two groups of Nikon Speedlights in close-up mode, or three groups (A, B, C) of compatible Speedlights in commander mode. In either mode, the commander manages flash output with exceptional precision, automatically delivering the light level dictated by the camera's metering systems and supporting automatic balanced fill-flash with compatible cameras. Further, the Nikon D200 and later models feature a built-in flash commander that allows the on-board flash to control the output of two groups of flash units remotely to a distance of 66 feet.

In use, the Flash Commander is remarkable because you can easily control the output and ratio between flashes and verify the results on the camera's LCD. With an assistant or attendee helping you, you can light scenes with multiple flash wirelessly and easily control the output of each flash so that you can shoot groups at the reception, or special moments like the first dance or cake cutting, with sophisticated TTL flash lighting.

57. Studio Flash Systems on Location

You may find it useful to have a number of studio flash heads. You can set these up for formals or tape the light stands to the floor and use them to light the reception. Either way, you will need enough power (at least 50 watt-seconds per head) to light large areas or allow you to work at small apertures at close distances. The most popular type of unit is the monolight, which has a self-contained power pack and usually has an on-board photo cell that triggers the unit to fire when it senses a flash burst. All you need is an electrical outlet and the flash can be positioned anywhere. Be

YOU CAN SET THESE UP FOR FORMALS OR TAPE THE LIGHT STANDS TO THE FLOOR AND USE THEM TO LIGHT THE RECEPTION.

Nikon SB-800

Mike Colón carries a small arsenal of Nikon SB-800 AF speedlights to every wedding. "I set them up around the dance floor for a dramatic backlight, or use them for my table shots," he says. "I'll throw some light on the table from behind with one unit, and have an on-camera SB-800 at minus two or three stops so it looks like the ambient light in the room hitting the table from the front."

Mike Colón used two SB-800 AF Speedlights to illuminate the bride and groom during their first dance.

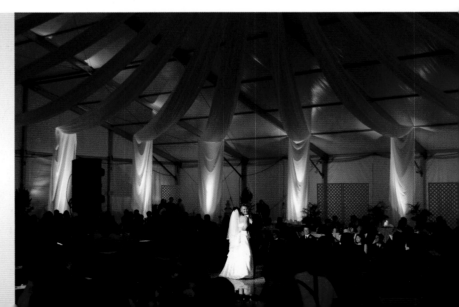

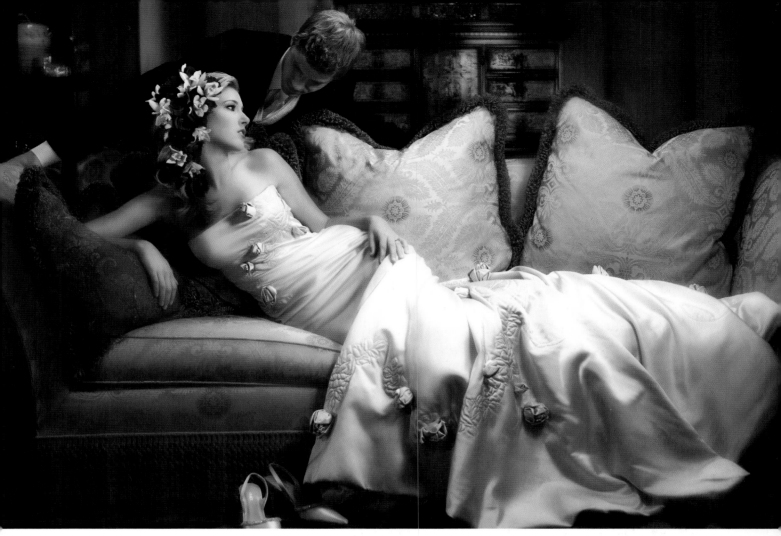

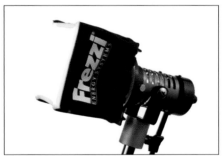

According to Bruce Dorn, this scene was the perfect opportunity to use a nifty little 12-volt Sun-Gun. With the appropriate diffusion, this setup is really quite simple and direct. Most Sun-Guns are based around 20- to 100-watt projector lamps and their undiffused beams, which, according to Dorn are "almost universally nasty." He always uses a mini-softbox or adds a layer of Lee Filters' No. 261 Full Tough Spun to improve the light's character. While there are a variety of brands to chose from, he prefers the dimmable Frezzi Mini-Fill units, which he uses with either 100-watt 3200K or 50-watt 4700K lamps. Dorn advises feathering the light onto your subject. He usually starts by wasting some of the illumination well out in front of the face, then slowly panning the beam back toward the subject until he likes both the look and the intensity. When dimming tungsten sources, Dorn notes that the color temperature will plummet as quickly as the output.

sure to take along plenty of gaffers' tape and extension cords. Tape everything in position securely in order to prevent accidents.

58. Use Umbrellas

Often, you will need to light an area, such as the dance floor. Using stationary umbrellas that are "slaved" to your camera or on-camera flash is an ideal way to accomplish this. When setting up, be sure to securely tape all cords and stands to the floor in as inconspicuous a manner as possible to prevent anyone from tripping over them.

Once positioned, focus the umbrellas so that you get even illumination across the area. To do that, use the modeling light to adjust the distance of the umbrella to the flash head until outer edges of the light core strike the outer edges of the umbrella. This is the optimal setting. If the umbrella is too close to the strobe, much of the beam of light is focused in the center portion of the umbrella, producing light with a "hot-spot" center. If the strobe is too far away from the umbrella surface, the beam of light is focused past the umbrella surface, wasting a good amount of light.

Feathering the light past the area you want illuminated will help more evenly light your scene, because you are using the edge of the light. Additionally, you can move the light source back so that is less intense overall but covers a wider area. The light will become harsher and less diffused the farther back you move it. Triggering is best accomplished with a radio transmitter set to fire only those strobes.

59. TRY HANDHELD VIDEO LIGHTS

Small handheld video light are a good addition to your location-photography kit. Perhaps the most useful video lights come from Lowel Light, a video and hot-light manufacturer. Lowel's 100-watt dimmable iD light, which is ultracompact, does not get too hot to manage and is ideal for hand-holding when your other hand is holding a camera. Barn doors are part of

For Bruce Dorn's photographic contribution to his daughter Carly's wedding, he rigged two 200-watt remotely-dimmable Mole-Richardson "InBetweenie" halogen solar-spots, which were piggy-backed with two radio-triggered and warmly-gelled Quantum T5d-R strobes.

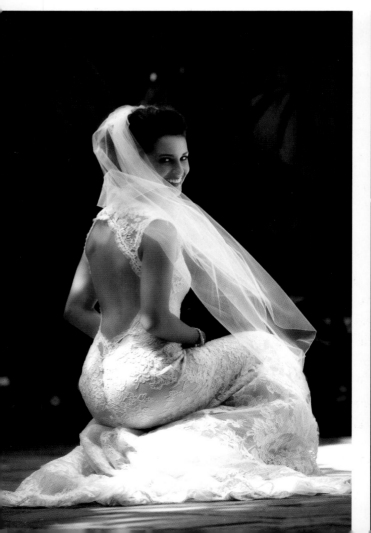
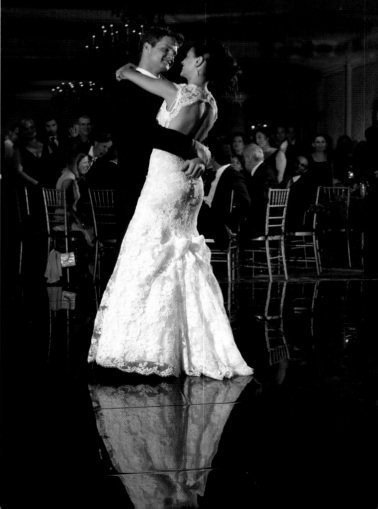

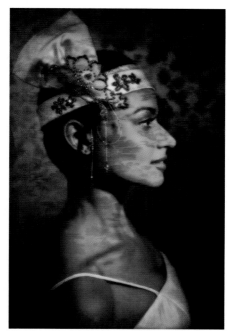

Australian wedding pro Yervant often uses handheld video lights to light his subject in dimly lit locales. He'll use an assistant to hold the light and feather its beam to attain the most dynamic lighting.

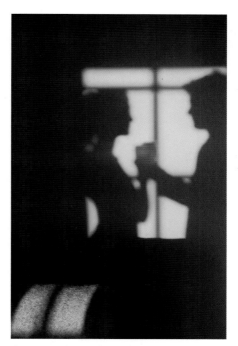

Getting to know the couple in advance will help ensure that they are completely relaxed with you and your camera. Photograph by Ray Prevost.

the kit and the light is crisp and bright and, more importantly, easily feathered to produce the desired on-location lighting effect.

David Williams uses video lights to augment existing light at his weddings. To bring the white balance back from tungsten to about 4500°K (slightly warmer than daylight), he glues a Cokin filter holder to the front of the light and places a medium blue filter (a 025 Cokin filter) in it. The result is a perfect warm fill light. For an even warmer effect, or if you are shooting indoors with tungsten lights, you can simply remove the filter.

David uses these units when shooting wide open, so they are usually just for fill or accent. They can also be used to provide what David calls a "kiss of light." For this effect, he holds the light above and to the side of the subject and feathers the beam back and forth while looking through the viewfinder. The idea is to produce just a little warmth and light on something that is backlit or lit nondescriptly. Alternately, David will use an assistant to hold two lights, which cancel out the shadows of one another. He often combines these in a flash-bracket arrangement with a handle. His video light has a palm grip attached to the bottom to make it very maneuverable, even when he has a camera in his other hand.

60. BEFRIEND THE COUPLE

Most successful wedding photographers get to know the couple and their families before the wedding so that everyone knows what to expect. This process can involve in-studio consultations, creating an engagement portrait (in which the photographer and couple actually work together), sending handwritten notes, communicating via e-mail, and talking on the phone. Alisha and Brook Todd, successful wedding photographers in the San Francisco area, send out a bottle of Dom Perignon and a hand-written note the day after the contract goes out, then follow it up with monthly phone calls to check in. The more familiar the couple is with the photographer, the better the pictures will be on the wedding day.

61. GET TO KNOW THE EVENT

Preparation is critical when photographing a once-in-a-lifetime event that is as complicated as a wedding. With lots of people, places, and events to document, getting all the details and formulating a plan will help ensure you're ready to capture every moment.

Begin by arranging a meeting with the couple at least one month before the wedding. Use this time to get all the details, formulate detailed plans, and get to know the couple in a relaxed setting. Make notes on the color scheme, the supplier of the flowers, the caterer, the band, and so on.

After the meeting, contact all of the vendors just to touch base. You may find out interesting details that will affect your timetable or how you make certain photos. Introduce yourself to the people at the various venues (including the minister, priest, or rabbi), and go back to the couple if there are any problems or if you have questions.

If you have not worked at the couples' venues before, try to visit them at the same times of day as the wedding and reception. That way, you can check the lighting, make notes of special locations, and catalog any potential problems. Also, you should make note of the walls and types of ceilings, particularly at the reception. This will affect your use of bounce flash. It is useful to produce an "A" list and a "B" list of locations. On the "A" list, note the best possible spots for your images; on the "B" list, select alternate locations in case your "A" locations don't work out on the wedding day.

Your initial meeting with the couple also gives them a chance to ask any questions of you that they may have. Discuss what you plan to photograph, and show them examples. Be sure to ask if they have any special requests or special guests who may be coming from far away—but avoid creating a list of "required" photographs; it may not be possible to adhere to one.

62. ENGAGEMENT PORTRAITS SMOOTH THE PATH

The engagement portrait, which has become a classic element of modern-day wedding coverage, is often used in newspapers and local magazines to

LEFT—One shouldn't necessarily expect great shots from the altar—but being prepared makes all the difference. After the ceremony, someone said something hysterical to the couple, and Marcus Bell was primed to get the shot. **RIGHT**—Marcus Bell arranged for the bride to exit the altar of this magnificent church through a side entrance, at which he would make a few formals before releasing the couple to go the reception. He didn't count on the hopelessly bored flower girls hanging out in his shot, but they added the perfect element.

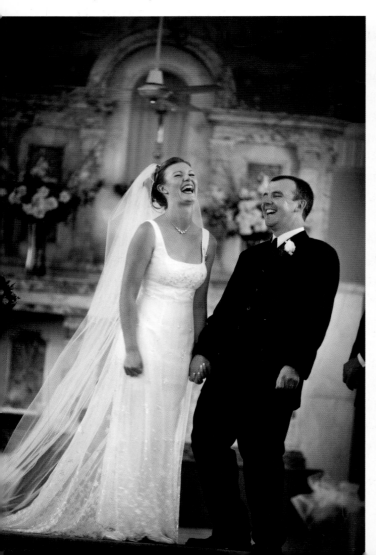

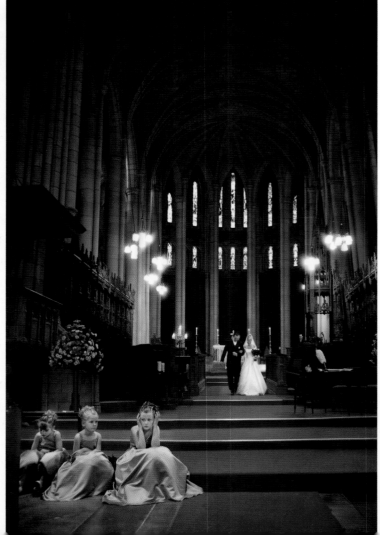

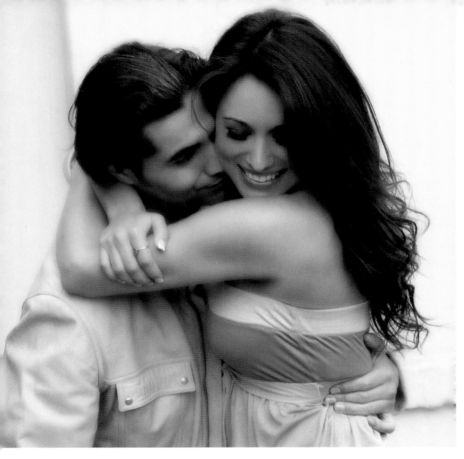
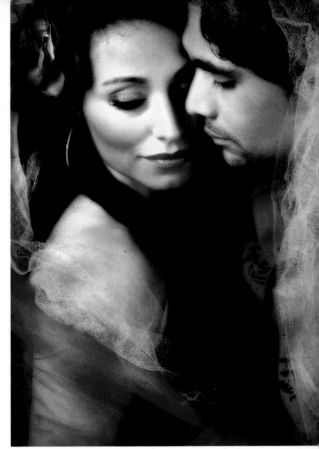

California photographer Jerry D is a big believer in the "free" engagement session because it gives the trio (bride, groom, and photographer) a chance to work together before the wedding day. And when they see his work, they are supremely confident in him as a friend and photographer. Jerry will often do a studio session and a location session on the same day so that he can get a variety of finished results.

announce the couple's wedding day. These portraits are generally made in advance of the wedding, providing the time needed to get something really spectacular. This pre-wedding session also allows the couple and the photographer to become familiar with each other, making the wedding-day photography much easier. After a successful engagement-portrait session, the photographer doesn't seem like an outsider at the wedding.

Most photographers offer this session at no charge, because it affords them two to three hours of bonding time with the couple. Engagement portraits may involve great creativity and intimacy and are often made in the photographer's studio or at some location that is special to the couple.

63. MAKE A BRIDAL PORTRAIT, TOO

According to Kevin Jairaj, doing a bridal session before the wedding is a great idea (and very profitable too!). It allows him to get to know the bride a lot better and to see what she is comfortable with in regard to her photos. It is also a great dress rehearsal for the bride as she can make sure that all parts of her dress fit just right and look exactly the way she wants.

Kevin always approaches his bridal sessions with the attitude that it's more like a fashion shoot. He tells his brides to "expect to be my model for a day and to prepare to have a lot of fun." During the session, he will do quite a variety of shots from very sexy and fashion-forward, to a few traditional ones to please Mom and Grandma. He offers some tips:

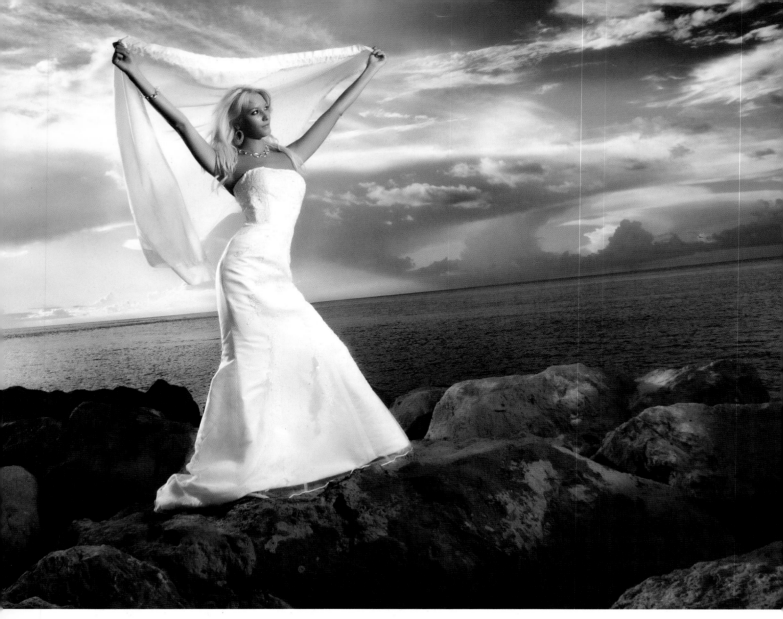

1. Tell the bride to have a glass of wine to relax before the session, as putting on the wedding dress comes with a few nerves.

2. Have the bride wear comfortable shoes (tennis shoes or flip flops) especially if you cannot see her shoes under her dress when she is standing. Having your bride get blisters while walking around in her heels is no way to have a productive shoot! For any shots sitting down you can simply have her put her heels on when you get to the spot.

3. Bring a white sheet or clean painter's plastic to place under the dress during some shots. This is the secret to not getting the dress dirty. Some brides are terrified to have their $10,000 dress get dirty before the wedding! Have her sit on the sheet or the plastic and then tuck it under her dress so that it doesn't show.

4. Have her bring friends to the session to help out with all the

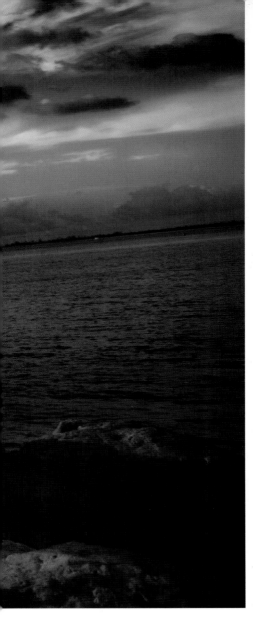

This coastal bridal portrait was created at about 3:00pm. Kevin Jairaj used a softbox, about six feet from the bride, to overpower the daylight and create a more flattering lighting pattern. According to Kevin, "I set the strobe in the softbox to almost full power so that I could overpower the sun and create some deep blue skies by slightly underexposing the background."

stuff (shoes, makeup, tissues, etc.). "Most brides seem to relax more when their friends are around," Kevin notes.

Kevin tries to do the bridal session about two months before the actual wedding, since the bride's weight, hair length, etc. will be pretty close to what it will be on the wedding day. Also, that allows him plenty of time to order and frame a print to be displayed at the reception. A typical bridal session will last about two to three hours.

64. HAVE A MASTER SCHEDULE

Planning is essential to a smooth wedding day. The couple should know that if there are delays, adjustments or deletions will have to be made to the requested pictures. Good planning and an understanding of exactly what the bride and groom want will help prevent any problems.

Inform the bride that you will arrive at the her home or hotel room (or wherever she is getting ready) at least 45 minutes to an hour before she leaves for the church. You should know how long it takes to drive from there to the ceremony, and leave in time to arrive at church at about the same time as (or a little before) the groom, who should arrive about a half-hour before the ceremony. At that time you can make portraits of the groom and his groomsmen and his best man while you wait for the bride and bridesmaids to arrive. (For more on photographs to take before the wedding, see pages 93–98.)

If the ceremony is to take place at a church or synagogue where you do not know the customs, make sure you visit the officiant beforehand. If you are unfamiliar with the customs, ask to attend another wedding as an observer. Such experiences will give you invaluable insight into how you will photograph the wedding. (For more on photographs to take at the ceremony, see page 99–101.)

Bear in mind that having a master schedule does not preclude massive scheduling changes. A good plan will only guarantee that you are prepared for the events as they are planned, not necessarily how they will actually unfold. Yet, the better your preparation and planning, the more adept you and your team will be at making last-minute adjustments.

65. LEARN EVERYBODY'S NAMES

Photography is not just about the images, it also involves people skills. Photographer Frank Frost believes that you should master the names of the key players. He says, "There can be twenty people in the wedding party and I'm able to call everybody by name. It makes a big impression and, by the end of the evening, everybody is my friend." At the very least, you should make a note of the parents' names, as well as the names of the bridesmaids, groomsmen, the best man, and maid of honor, so that you can address each. If you are not good at memorizing names, you must practice.

66. WORK WITH AN ASSISTANT

An assistant is invaluable at the wedding. He or she can run interference for you, change or download CompactFlash (CF) cards, organize guests for a group shot, help you by taking flash readings and predetermining exposure, tape light stands and cords securely with duct tape, and tackle a thou-

TO FUNCTION EFFECTIVELY, YOUR ASSISTANT MUST BE TRAINED IN YOUR POSING AND LIGHTING TECHNIQUES.

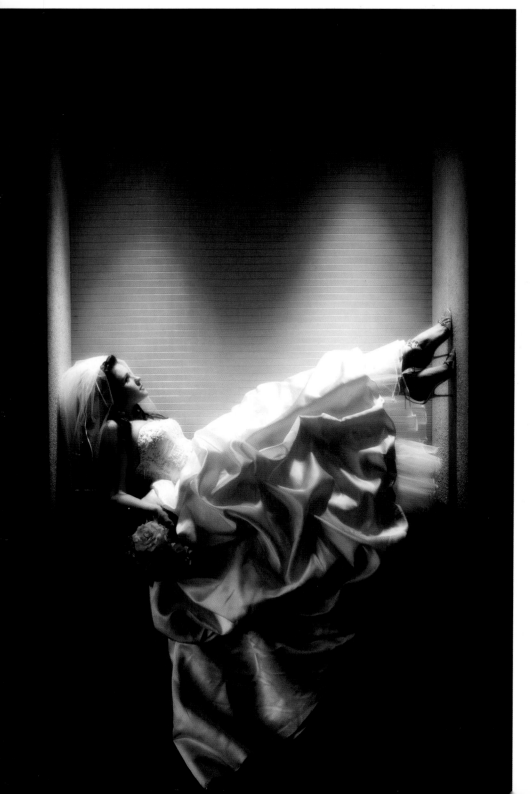

In this hotel bridal portrait, Kevin used the can lights straight above the bride to illuminate her face and produce nice detail in her dress. (Most hotels have little spots like these over the desk area.) According to Kevin Jairaj, "The bride thought I was crazy at first for asking her to sit up here, but she trusted me enough and it ended up being her favorite shot from the whole session!"

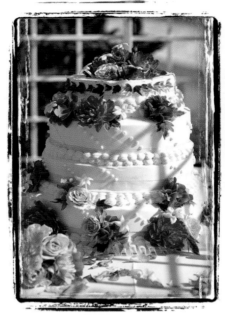

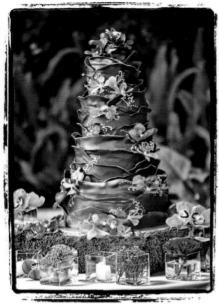

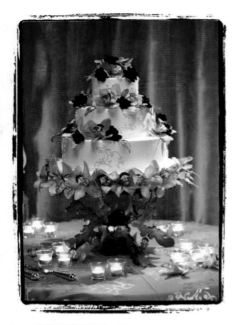

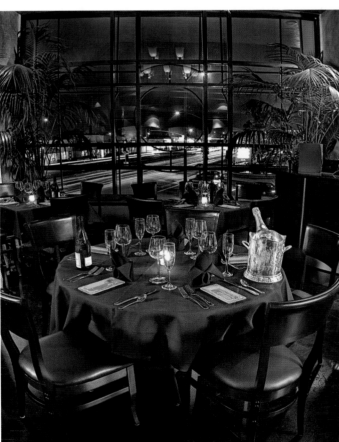

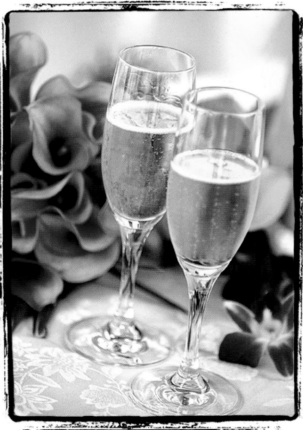

Marc Weisberg is very sensitive to the details of all his weddings. This is where it pays to be more than just a wedding photographer—to be able to light small products on location, to mix and control various light sources, and to record a myriad of the fine details of the day.

sand other chores. Your assistant can survey your backgrounds looking for unwanted elements—and even become a moveable light stand by holding your secondary flash or reflectors.

To function effectively, your assistant must be trained in your posing and lighting techniques. The wedding day is not the time to find out that

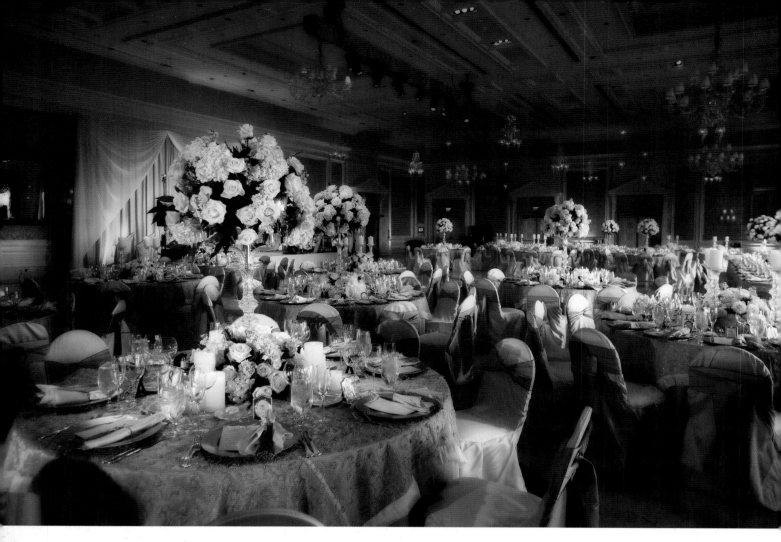

the assistant either doesn't understand or—worse yet, *approve of*—your techniques. You should both be on the same page; a good assistant will be able to anticipate your next need and keep you on track for upcoming shots.

Most assistants go on to become full-fledged wedding photographers. After you've developed confidence in an assistant, he or she can help with the photography, particularly at the reception, when there are too many things going on at once for one person to cover. Most assistants try to work for several different wedding photographers to broaden their experience. It's not a bad idea to employ more than one assistant so that if you get a really big job you can use both of them—or if one is unavailable, you have a backup assistant.

Assistants also make good security guards. I have heard many stories of gear "disappearing" at weddings. An assistant is another set of eyes who can make it a priority to safeguard the equipment.

67. DRESS FOR SUCCESS
Photographer Ken Sklute says it's important to select your wedding-day attire carefully. A suit or slacks and a sports jacket are fine for men. For

Tom Muñoz use a 24mm lens and a mix of window light and tungsten room lighting to create this beautiful shot of the reception before the guests arrived.

women, business attire works well. Remember that you have to lug equipment and move freely, though, so don't wear restrictive clothing. Many wedding photographers (men *and* women) wear a tux for formal weddings.

68. AT THE BRIDE'S HOUSE/HOTEL ROOM

Typically, wedding-day coverage begins with the bride getting ready. Find out what time you may arrive (ideally, about an hour before the bride leaves for the church) and be there a little early. You may have to wait a bit—there are a million details for the bride and her helpers to attend to—but don't just stand around. Instead, look for opportunities to create still lifes or family shots. You may even suggest that the bride's family arrange for the flowers to be delivered early and use the time to set up an attractive still life for the album while you wait.

When you get the okay to enter the bride's room, realize that it may be tense in there. Try to blend in and observe. Look for shots as they present themselves, particularly with the mother and daughter or the bridesmaids.

Getting the bride ready to go is often an operation requiring many hands. This is a fun time as everyone feels like they are helping to ready the bride for her big moment. Photograph by Greg Gibson.

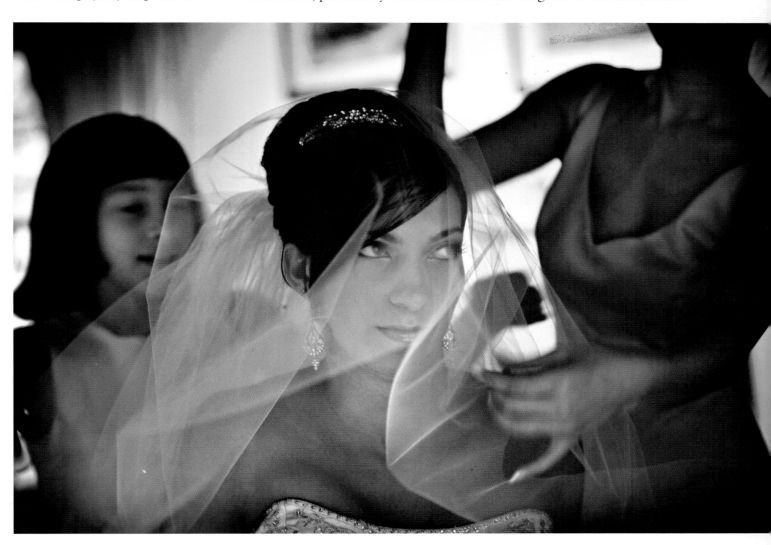

69. PHOTOGRAPHING THE BRIDE'S ATTIRE

The Wedding Dress. In most cases, the bride will spend more money on her wedding dress and more time on her appearance than for any other occasion in her entire life. The photographs you make will be a permanent record of how beautiful she looked on her wedding day.

Formal wedding dresses often include flowing trains. It is important to get several full-length portraits of the full train, draped out in front in a circular fashion or flowing behind. Include all of the train, as these may be the only photographs of her full wedding gown. If making a formal group

THE PHOTOGRAPHS YOU MAKE WILL BE A PERMANENT RECORD OF HOW BEAUTIFUL SHE LOOKED ON HER WEDDING DAY.

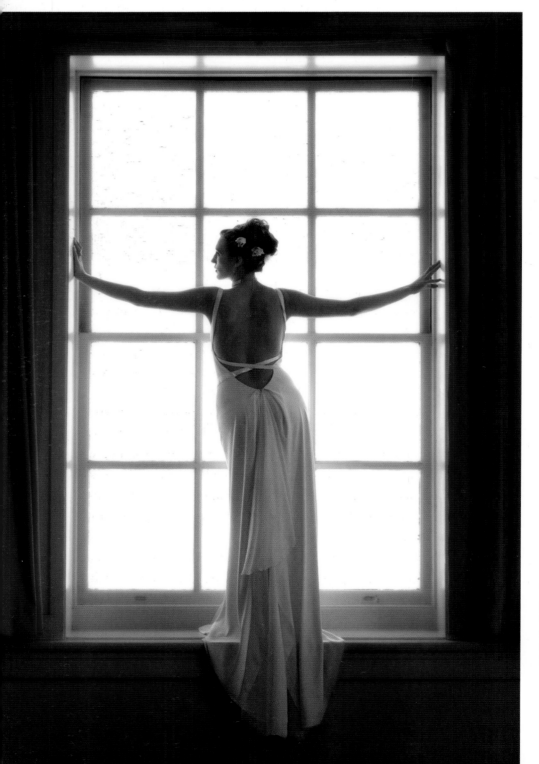

To show off the full dress and train, the photographer might pose a bride on a window sill so that the full line of the dress can be appreciated. Photograph by Jerry Ghionis. The image was made by window light with a Canon EOS 5D and 50mm lens.

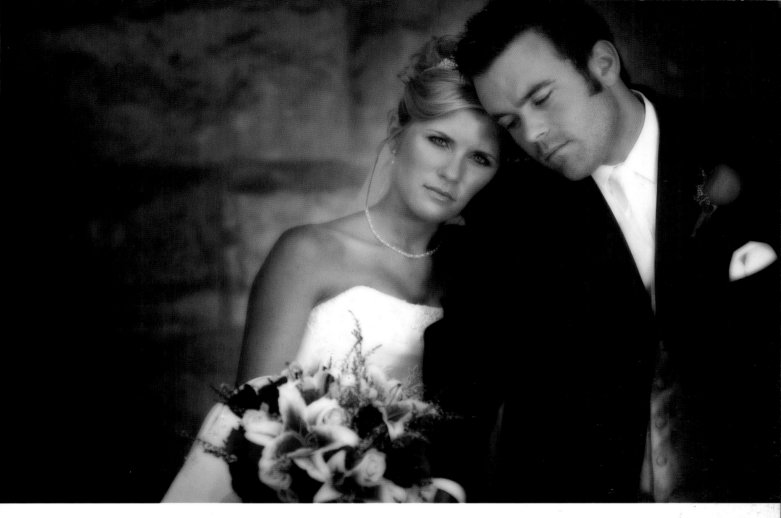

This is both a formal portrait of the bride and groom and a beautiful rendering of the bouquet. The couple's shapes form a perfect triangle, which yields a very pleasing composition. Photography by Jeff and Julia Woods.

portrait, this might also be an appropriate time to reveal the full train pulled to the front. To make the train look natural, pick it up and let it gently fall to the ground.

Do not ignore the back of the dress. Designers often incorporate as much style and elegance into the back of the dress as the front. Be sure to capture nice images of the bridesmaids' gowns as well.

The Bouquet. Make sure a large bouquet does not overpower your composition, particularly in your formal portrait of the bride. The bride should look comfortable holding the bouquet, and it should be an important and colorful element in the composition. For best effect, the bride should hold the bouquet in front of her with her hands behind it. It should be held high enough to put a slight bend in her elbows, keeping her arms slightly separated from her body.

The Veil. Make sure to get some close-ups of the bride through her veil. It acts like a diffuser and produces romantic, beautiful results. For this shot, the lighting should be from the side rather than head-on to avoid shadows on the bride's face caused by the patterned mesh. Many photographers use the veil as a compositional element in their portraits. To do this, lightly stretch the veil so that the corners slant down toward the lower cor-

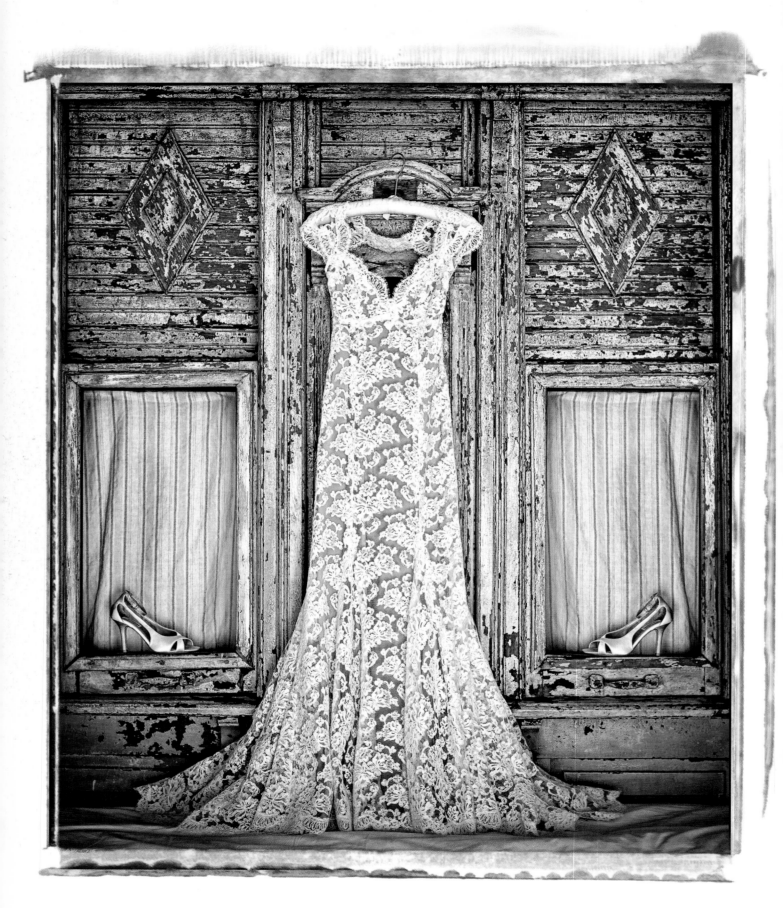

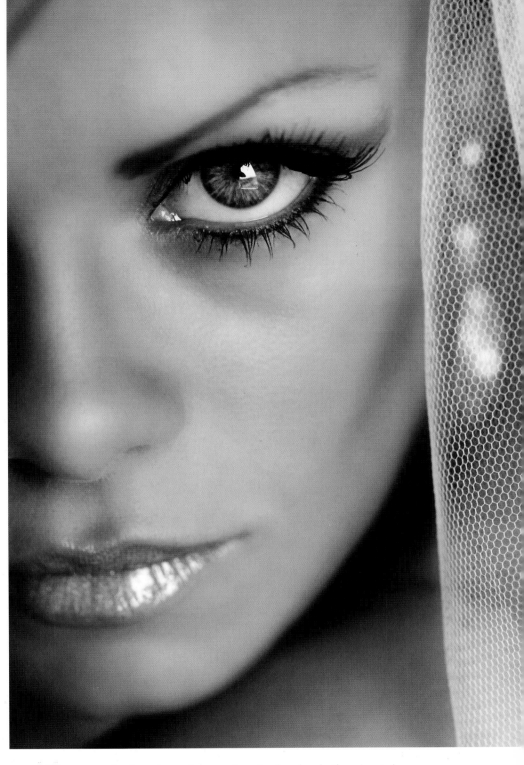

FACING PAGE—This is a remarkable detail shot of the wedding dress composed like a still life by Marc Weisberg. The original image was made with a Canon EOS-1D Mark III and EF 24–70mm f/2.8L USM lens at ISO 800. In RAW processing, the image was vignetted and its brightness and contrast were bumped up considerably. Then, it was treated with a LucisArt filter in Photoshop. RIGHT—Jerry Ghionis moved in close to reveal the unusual emerald color of this bride's eyes.

ners of the portrait, forming a loose triangle that leads the viewer's eyes up to the bride's eyes.

70. WORKING WITH LATE BRIDES

If the bride is late, don't add to her stress by holding things up—especially when her guests are waiting. Simply make a series of photojournalistic images of her arrival and make the other needed shots later in the day.

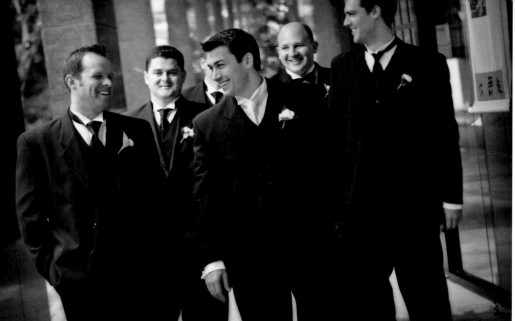

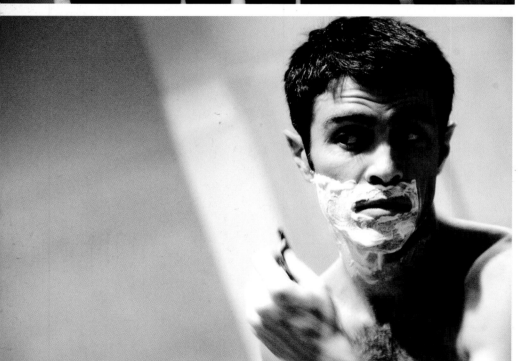

71. Working with the Guys

You do, of course, want to photograph the groom before the wedding. Some grooms are nervous, others are gregarious—like it's any other day. Regardless, there are ample picture opportunities before anyone else arrives. It's also a great opportunity to do formal portraits of the groom, the groom and his dad, and the groom and his best man. A three-quarter-length portrait is a good choice—and you can include the architecture of the venue to really set the scene. When photographing men, always check that the ties are properly knotted. If they are wearing vests, make sure that they are correctly buttoned and that the bottom button is undone.

72. COVERING THE CEREMONY

The first step when photographing a wedding is to learn the policies of the venue. At some churches you may be able to move around freely, at others you may only be able to take photographs from the back, in still others you may be offered the chance to go into a gallery or the balcony. You should also be prepared for the possibility that you may not be able to make pictures at all during the ceremony.

Whatever photography policies the church may dictate, you must be discrete during the ceremony. Nobody wants to hear the "ca-chunk" of

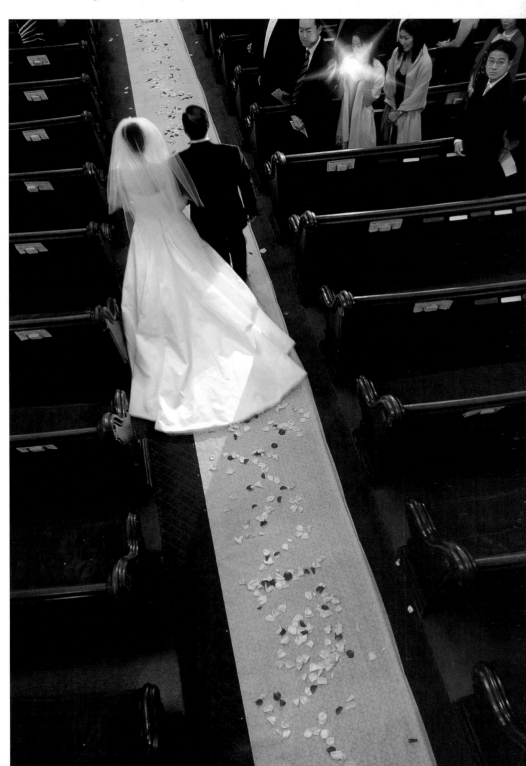

If there is a choir loft or balcony at the church, try to capture the bride and groom's entrance from above. This image was created by Joe Buissink. Note the serendipitous flash that went off at the exact moment Joe made the exposure.

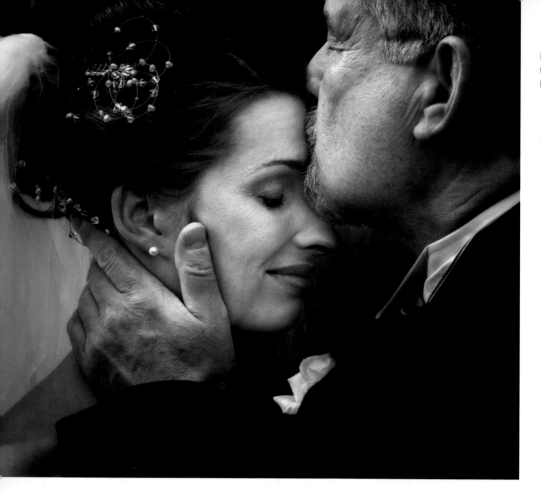

Be on the lookout for tender moments as the ceremony draws near. Photograph by Marcus Bell.

camera or see a blinding flash as the couple exchange their vows. It's better by far to work from a distance with a tripod- or monopod-mounted DSLR, and to work by available light, which will provide a more intimate feeling to the images. Work quietly and unobserved—in short, be invisible.

Some of the events you will need to cover are: the bridesmaids and flower girls entering the church; the bride entering the church; the parents being escorted in; the bride's dad "giving her away;" the first time the bride and groom meet at the altar; the minister or priest talking with them; the ring exchange; the exchange of vows; the kiss; the bride and groom turning to face the assembly; the bride and groom coming up the aisle; and any number of two dozen variations—plus all the surprises along the way. Note that this scenario applies only to a Christian wedding. Every religion has its own customs and traditions that you need to be thoroughly familiar with before the wedding.

BE PART OF THE TEAM

As the photographer, you are part of the group of wedding specialists who will ensure that the bride and groom have a great day. Be friendly and helpful to all of the people on the team—the minister, the limo driver, the wedding coordinator, the banquet manager, the band members, the florist, and other vendors involved in the wedding. They are great sources of referrals. Get the addresses of their companies so that you can send them a print of their specialty after the wedding.

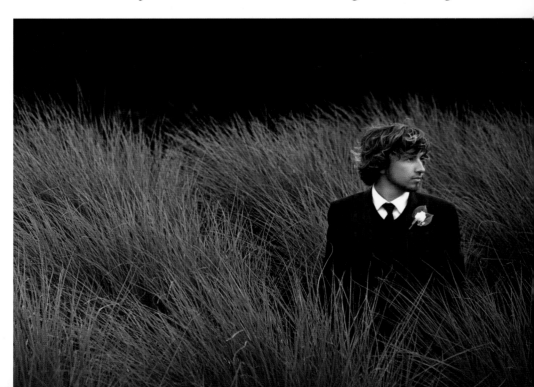

The rice toss (or, in this case, the rose petal toss) is one shot you want to have well covered from several angles. If you work with an assistant, choose a different location from which to capture the fleeting event. Don't be afraid to choreograph the event, as you'll only get one chance to make a great shot. Photograph by Jeff and Julia Woods.

73. LEAVING THE CHURCH

Predetermine the composition and exposure and be ready and waiting as the couple exits the church. If guests are throwing confetti or rice, don't be afraid to choreograph the event in advance. You can alert guests to get ready and "release" on your count. Using a slow ($\frac{1}{30}$ second) shutter speed and flash, you will freeze the couple and the rice, but the moving objects will have a blurred edge. If you'd rather just let it happen, do a burst sequence at the camera's fastest setting and with a wide-angle-to-short-telephoto zoom. Be alert for the unexpected, and consider having a second shooter cover events like this to better your odds of getting the key picture.

74. TACKLE THE FORMAL PORTRAITS QUICKLY

Following the ceremony, you should be able to steal the bride and groom for a brief time. Limit yourself to ten minutes, or you will be taking too much of their time and the others in attendance will get a little edgy. Most photographers will get what they need in less than ten minutes.

In addition to formal portraits of the couple, their first pictures as man and wife, you should try to make whatever group shots the couple has asked for, including portraits with the wedding party and the couple's families. Regardless of your style of coverage, these are pictures that will be desired by all. Be aware of shots that the bride may not have requested, but expects to see. The bride with her new parents and the groom with his are great shots, but are not ones that will necessarily be "on the list." If there are too many "must" shots to do in a short time, arrange to do some after the ceremony and some at the reception. This can be all thought out beforehand.

Keep in mind that the wedding day is usually a tense time. There is a surplus of emotion and people tend to wear those emotions on their sleeves. Your demeanor and professionalism should be a calming and reassuring

Make sure to get a great portrait of the groom. Photograph by Jerry Ghionis.

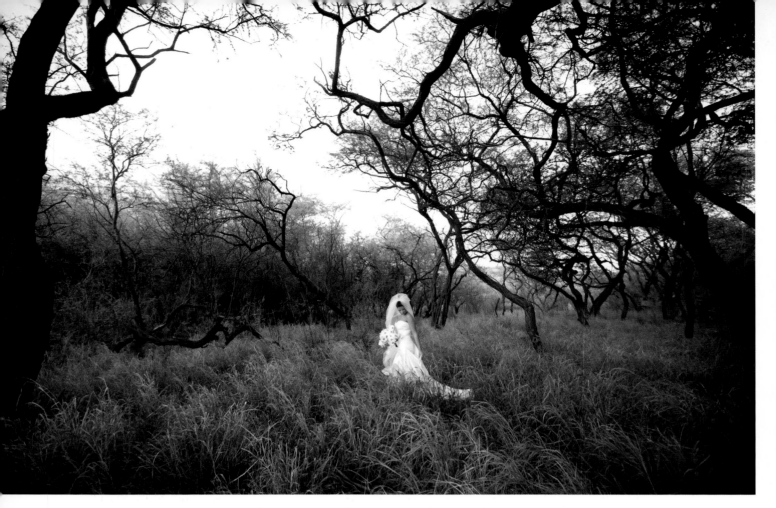

presence, especially to the bride. Be calm and positive, be funny and light-hearted—and above all, don't force the situation. If you can see that demanding to make a picture is going to really upset people, have the will power to hold off until later. Remember that positive energy is contagious, and can usually save a sticky situation.

Joe Buissink made this elegant bridal portrait, purposely keeping the bride's size small in the frame so he could create the illusion that the naked winter trees, darkened in printing, were rising up around the bride as if to protect her.

75. HAVE FUN WITH THE WEDDING PARTY

This is one "formal" group that does not have to be formal. I have seen wedding party portraits with the bride, groom, bridesmaids, and grooms-men doing a conga line down the beach, dresses held high out of the water and the men's pant legs rolled up. And I have seen elegant, formal pyramid arrangements, where every bouquet and every pose is identical and beautiful. It all depends on your client and your tastes. Most opt for boy–girl arrangements, with the bride and groom somewhere central in the image. As with the bridal portrait (see technique 77), the bridesmaids should be in front of the groomsmen in order to highlight their dresses.

76. POSING THE BRIDAL PORTRAITS

Take plenty of photographs of the bride to show the dress from all angles. To display the dress beautifully, the bride must stand well. Although you may only be taking a three-quarter-length or head-and-shoulders portrait, start the pose at the feet. When you arrange the bride's feet with one foot forward of the other, the shoulders will naturally be at their most flattering, one higher than the other. Have her stand at an angle to the lens, with her weight on her back foot and her front knee slightly bent. The most feminine position for her head is to have it turned and tilted toward the higher shoulder. This places the entire body in an attractive S-curve, a classic pose.

HAVE THE BRIDE HOLD HER BOUQUET IN THE HAND ON THE SAME SIDE OF HER BODY AS THE FOOT THAT IS EXTENDED.

Have the bride hold her bouquet in the hand on the same side of her body as the foot that is extended. If the bouquet is held in the left hand, the right arm should come in to meet the other at wrist level. She should hold her bouquet a bit below waist level to show off the waistline of the dress, which is an important part of the dress design.

77. PHOTOGRAPHING THE BRIDE AND GROOM

Generally speaking, portraits of the couple should be created using romantic poses, with the couple looking at each other. While a formal pose or two is advisable, most couples will also enjoy some more natural and emotional portraits. Be sure to highlight the dress, as it is a crucial element to formal portraits. Take pains to show the form as well as the details of the dress and train, if the dress has one.

Details are important, so position the couple carefully. Place the bride closest to the camera (in front of the groom) to keep her in proper perspective and allow her dress to be seen. Have the groom place his arm around her with his hand in the middle of her back. Have them lean in toward each other, with their weight on their back feet and a slight bend to their forward knees.

The rings are as important as any other detail shot in the wedding album, especially when the image is as nice as this one by Joe Buissink. Joe used a Canon EOS 5D and an EF 50mm f/2.5 Compact Macro lens. The image was shot to isolate the shallow band of focus across the front-facing surface of the rings. The bold lead-in lines are a pattern on a linen napkin.

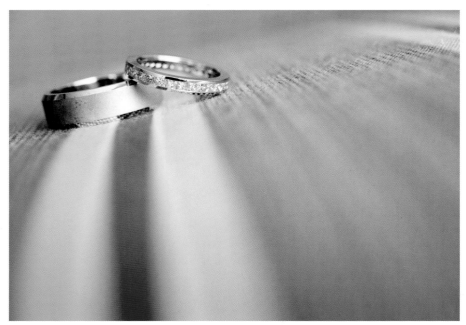

78. DISPLAY THE RINGS

The bride and groom usually love their new rings and want a shot that includes them. A close-up of the couple's hands displaying the rings makes a great detail image in the album. You can use any type of attractive pose, but remember that hands are difficult to pose. If you want a really close-up image of the rings, you will also need a macro lens, and you will probably have to light the scene with flash—unless you make the shot outdoors or in good light.

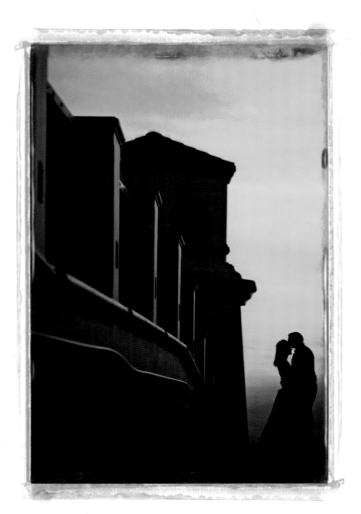

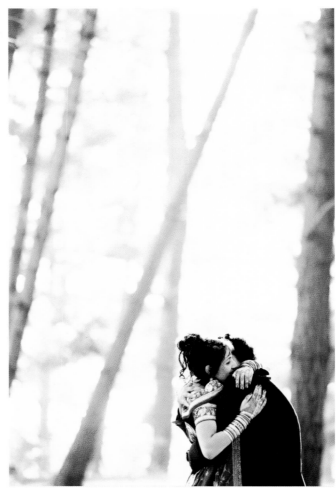

79. Capture A Kiss

Whether you set it up, which you may have to do, or wait for it to occur naturally, be sure to get the bride and groom kissing at least once. These are favorite shots and you will find many uses for them in the album. For the best results, get a good vantage point and make sure you adjust your camera angle so neither person obscures the other.

80. Taking Venue Shots

Whenever possible, try to make a photograph of the reception site before the guests arrive. Photograph one table in the foreground and be sure to include the floral and lighting effects. Also, photograph a single place setting and a few other details. The bride will love them, and you'll find use for them in the album design. The caterers and other vendors will also appreciate a print that reflects their fine efforts. Some photographers try to include the bride and groom in the scene, which can be tricky. Their presence does, however, add to the shot. Before the guests enter the reception area, for instance, Ken Sklute often photographs the bride and groom dancing slowly in the background and it is a nice touch.

LEFT—Some alone time with the bride and groom can yield fabulous shots on the day of the wedding. Marc Weisberg made this shot at sunset, with the sky backlighting the architecture and the couple. **RIGHT**—Your coverage should include as many shots of the bride and groom embracing and kissing as you can get. You'd be surprised at how often this integral scene gets neglected or omitted. Photography by Johannes Van Kan of Flax Studio in Christchurch, New Zealand.

81. DOCUMENT THE RECEPTION

The reception calls upon all of your skills and instincts. Things happen quickly, so don't get caught with an important event coming up and only two frames left on your CF card! Fast zooms and fast telephoto lenses paired with fast film or high ISO settings will give you the best chance to work unobserved. Often, the reception is best lit with a number of corner-mounted umbrellas, triggered by your on-camera flash or radio remote. That way, anything within the perimeter of your lights can be photographed by strobe. Be certain you meter various areas within your lighting perimeter so that you know what your exposure is everywhere on the floor.

The reception is all about the couple and guests having a great time, so be cautious about intruding upon events. Try to observe the flow of the reception and anticipate the individual events before they happen. As the re-

> **DON'T GET CAUGHT WITH AN IMPORTANT EVENT COMING UP AND ONLY TWO FRAMES LEFT ON YOUR CF CARD!**

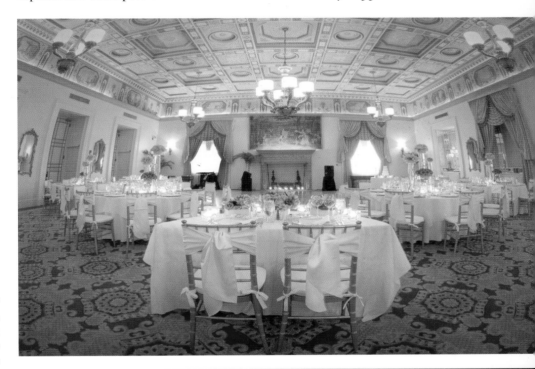

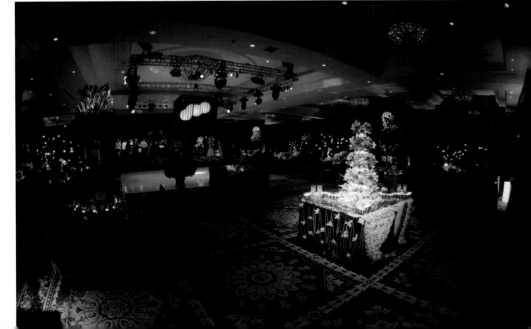

TOP—Jeff Kolodny does a masterful job of photographing the venue prior to the reception. Here he used a Nikon D200 and 10.5mm fisheye lens. With the camera tripod-mounted, he photographed the scene for 30 seconds at f/22, to extend the depth of field to cover the entire room. His white balance was set to automatic, but he warmed the scene in RAW file processing to bring out the delicate pinks and yellows. He also lowered the contrast in processing so he could better deal with the blown out windows at the far end of the room. The original scene was shot at ISO 100. **BOTTOM**—Joe Photo shoots every venue before the guests arrive to show of the opulence and beauty of the room. He always remembers to send the various vendors prints of the room and place settings afterwards as part of his gregarious customer service.

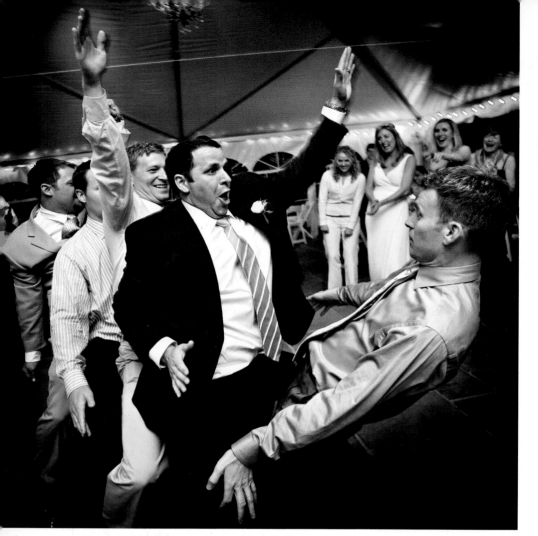

The reception is filled with great photo opportunities, especially if you have the reflexes of a first-rate photojournalist like Greg Gibson. Greg made this image with a Canon EOS-1D Mark II N and EF 16–35mm f/2.8L USM lens at 16mm. He lit the image with bounce flash off the white tent surface that served as a ceiling.

ception goes on and guests relax, the opportunities for great pictures will increase. Be sure to remain aware of the bride and groom all the time, as well; after all, they are the central players.

Be prepared for the scheduled events at the reception—the bouquet toss, removing the garter, the toasts, the first dance, and so on. If you have done your homework, you will know where and when each of these events will take place, and you will have prepared to light it and photograph it. You should also coordinate your efforts with the person in charge, usually the wedding planner or banquet manager. He or she can run interference for you, as well as cue you when certain events are about to occur, often not letting the event begin until you are ready.

I have watched Joe Photo work a reception and it is an amazing sight. He often uses his Nikon D1X and flash in bounce mode and works quickly

TABLE SHOTS

Table shots don't usually turn out well, are rarely ordered, and are tedious to make. If your couple absolutely wants table shots, ask them to accompany you from table to table. That way they can greet all of their guests, and it will make the posing quick and painless. As an alternative to table shots, you may also want to suggest one big group portrait that encompasses nearly everyone at the reception.

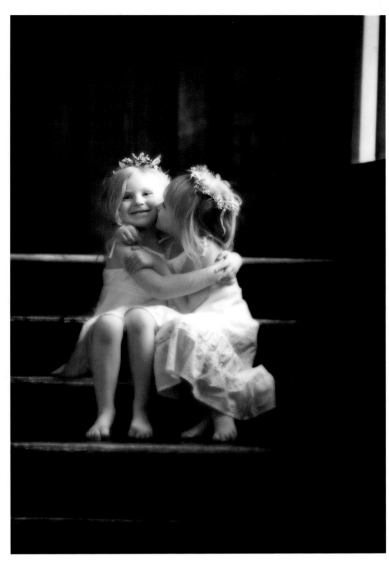

The bride will appreciate some shots of the little ones in the wedding party. The children are usually selected because they are relatives or somehow close to the family, so they will be a definite part of the wedding album. Kids can also be great photo subjects; they are usually thrilled with the pageantry of the wedding day and tend to be hams in front of the camera. Photograph by Jeff and Julia Woods.

and quietly. His Nikon Speedlite is outfitted with a small forward-facing internal reflector that redirects some of the bounce flash directly onto his subject, making the flash both main and fill light at once. If he is observed and noticed, he'll often walk over and show the principals the image on the LCD, offer some thoughtful compliment about how good they all look, and quickly move on. Other times he just shoots, observes, and shoots some more. His intensity and concentration at the reception are keen and he comes away with priceless images—the rewards of good work habits.

82. THE FIRST DANCE

When documenting the first dance, one trick you can use is to tell the couple beforehand, "Look at me and smile." That will keep you from having to circle the couple on the dance floor until you get both of them looking at you for the "first dance" shot. Or you can tell them, "Just look at each other and don't worry about me, I'll get the shot."

Often, photographers will photograph the first dance using the available light (often spotlights) on the dance floor. This is possible with fast lenses and fast ISOs. Just as frequently, the photographer will use flash and a slow shutter speed to record the ambient light in the room and the surrounding faces watching the couple's first dance. The flash will freeze the couple but there is often some blurring due to the slow shutter speed needed to capture the people only lit by ambient light.

83. THE BOUQUET TOSS

The bouquet toss is one of the more memorable shots at any wedding reception. Whether you're a photojournalist or traditionalist, this shot looks best when it's spontaneous. You need plenty of depth of field, which almost dictates a wide-angle lens. You'll want to show not only the bride but also the expectant faces in the background. Although you can use available light, the shot is usually best done with two flashes—one on the bride and one on the ladies waiting for the bouquet. Your timing has to be excellent, as the bride will often "fake out" the group just for laughs. This might fake

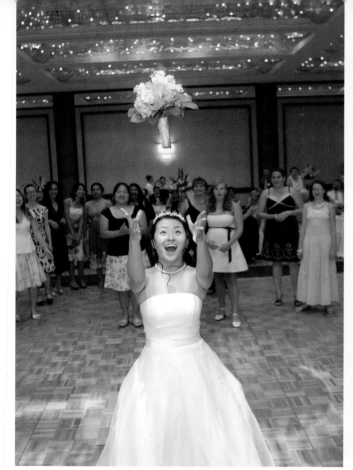
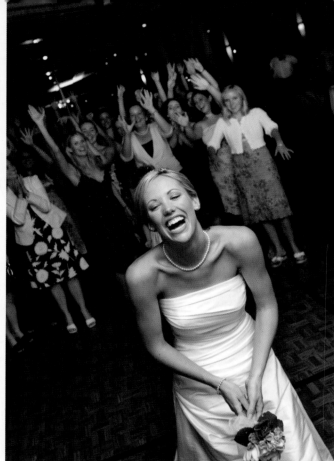

you out, as well. Try to get the bouquet as it leaves the bride's hands and before it is caught—and if your flash recycles fast enough, get a shot of the lucky lady who catches it.

84. TRAVELING TO DESTINATION WEDDINGS

Gene Higa does destination weddings and is on the road about three weeks out of every month. He travels with multiple Tamrac and Lowepro roller/backpack bags, which are certified to fit in the overhead compartment of any aircraft. Because Gene may have to go from a roller to a backpack in seconds, his bags need to be versatile. His equipment consists of two Canon EOS 5D bodies, two Canon EOS-1D Mark II bodies, and a Canon EOS 20D for backup. His lenses include a 15mm f/2.8 fisheye, a 14mm f/2.8 lens, a 24–70mm f/2.8 lens, a 24–105mm IS f/4.0 lens, a 50mm f/1.0 lens, two 70–200mm IS f/2.8 lenses, and two 16–35mm f/2.8 lenses. Gene also packs two 580EX flashes, 30 GB in Lexar and SanDisk Extreme CF cards, two Quantum battery packs, rechargeable AA batteries, Canon battery packs, and power adapters.

As long as he has an Internet connection, Gene can upload images to his lab. The prints are then delivered to his studio within a week of returning home. Gene also posts the images on his website so that they are ready to be viewed by the time the guests and couple return home. This approach

LEFT—An image of the bouquet toss is desirable for most weddings. Photograph by Regina and Denis Zaslavets. **RIGHT**—The bride often tries to "fake out" the ladies when tossing her bouquet. Here Mark Cafeiro captured this lovely bride in the middle of a belly laugh after just such a trick. Mark fired a bounce flash, held just to the right of the camera, at the bride and relied on enough ambient light to light the waiting brides-to-be. He stood on a chair to get above the scene for a better overall view.

has great sales impact because the wedding and the vacation are still fresh in their minds.

He edits with iView Media Pro, and he creates galleries using Troy Winder's Pickpic (www.pickpic.com), which gives guests the option to purchase prints online.

85. BACK UP AND REFORMAT

It is extremely important to back up your original (source) files before you reuse your CF cards. Some photographers shoot an entire job on a series of cards and take them back to the studio prior to performing any backup. Others opt to download, back up, and reformat cards throughout the day. This is a question of preference and security. Many photographers who shoot with a team of shooters train their assistants to perform these opera-

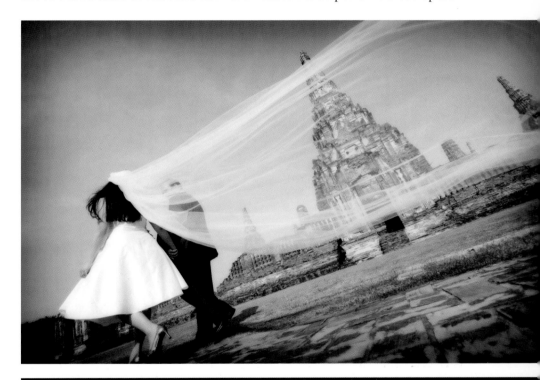

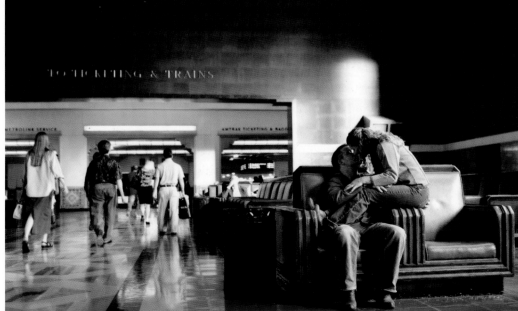

Part of the job of an international wedding photographer like Gene Higa is to incorporate exotic locales into the wedding pictures—but without the images looking like postcards.

tions to guarantee the images are safe and in hand before anyone leaves the wedding. (*Note:* If you opt for this policy, complete training is essential. A good friend of mine, who shall remain nameless, asked his assistant to download and reformat the cards at the wedding only to find out later that the cards had been reformatted but the image files had not been saved. There were no wedding pictures except for the cards still in the cameras.)

A good rule of thumb is to backup the files to CDs or DVDs as soon as possible. Avoid reformatting the CF cards until that has been done and verified. After you backup your source files, it's a good idea to erase all of the images from your CF cards and then reformat them. It simply isn't enough to delete the images, because extraneous data may remain on the card causing data interference. After reformatting, you're ready to use the CF card again.

86. DAN DOKE'S WEDDING WORKFLOW

Dan Doke is an award-winning wedding photographer who shoots numerous high-end weddings each year. On an average wedding day, Dan will work roughly eight hours with one assistant. Dan shoots the important shots, while his assistant helps with everything else—holding additional lighting, taking candid photographs and doing whatever is necessary. Dan works quickly and unobtrusively, only stepping in when necessary to make sure that everyone is in place.

Dan Doke made this beautiful and quiet portrait of the bride with his EF 85mm f/1.2L II USM lens and Canon EOS 1D Mark II. Because Dan uses an assistant for all of his weddings, he had someone to position a reflector precisely to light the frontal planes of the bride's face. Careful shading and vignetting in Photoshop completed the image.

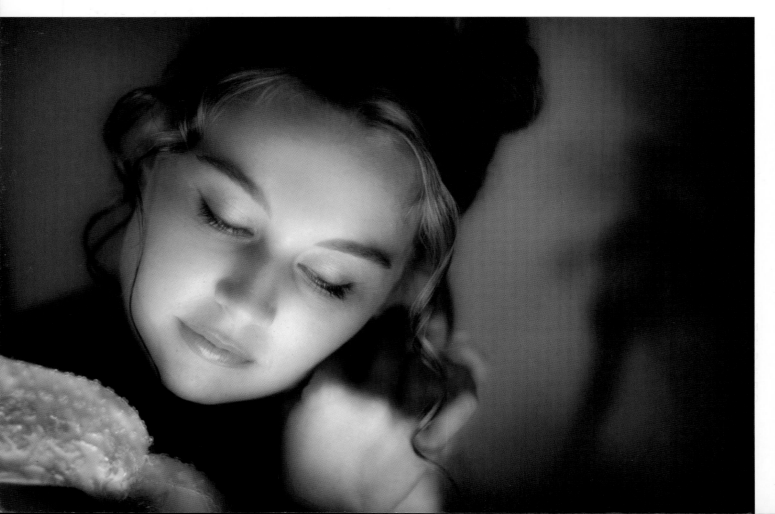

The day after the wedding, Dan joins his team in the studio and downloads the cards. He says, "I have a 1.5 TB computer with five drives, and I make copies onto two of them. I then drag files onto my server for backup and then onto DVDs. This gives me files in four areas." Within a week, his studio staff goes through all the images and picks the best shots. Some edits are done in Photoshop and then uploaded to Flip Albums so the bride can make selections.

Dan supervises all the work and consistently strives to produce the highest quality albums. For his albums, he uses PictoBooks, which he regards as "the best I've ever seen."

87. MIKE COLÓN'S WIFI WORKFLOW

Today's wedding clients expect immediacy. They aren't content with seeing proofs four weeks after the honeymoon. As a result, Mike Colón has revised his wedding workflow so that he can deliver wedding photos at the wedding reception—even photos taken during the reception.

To do this, Mike has each of his Nikon DSLRs fitted with a Nikon WT-1A wireless transmitter. As he shoots, the WT-1A automatically sends each frame to an Apple laptop, which comes with a built-in WiFi transceiver. It takes about two seconds for each image to transfer. At the same time, the images are still being written to the CF cards in the camera as backup.

During the ceremony, Mike's assistant (with the PowerBook) stays within transmitting range. This is typically about a hundred feet, although the optional Nikon WA-E1 extended antenna can transmit up to 450 feet from the camera. The assistant then checks the images as they are being shot in real time. Once he has a good number of images, Colón's assistant begins to create a slideshow. Near the end of the reception, Mike then uses a digital projector to produce a show for the guests. Images captured right

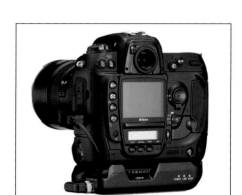

Nikon WT-2A transmitter on the D2X body. Images can be so quickly downloaded and ramped up for projection that wedding guests cannot believe their eyes.

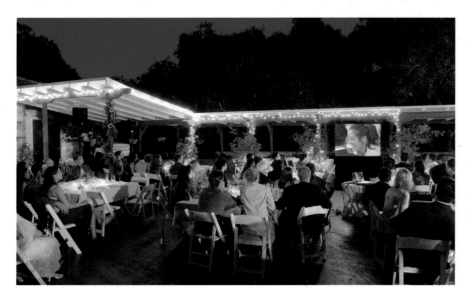

Here you see Mike Colón's elaborate WiFi setup. The assistant with the laptop is near the center of the photograph and the seated guests can't take their eyes off the projected images. Photograph by Mike Colón.

up to the start of the slide show can be incorporated into the presentation. Mike says the surprise of seeing the images immediately really delights both the guests and the bride and groom. Not surprisingly, he finds the spontaneity often makes guests more likely to order prints. If it's not possible to project the slide show, he will show the images directly on the PowerBook.

While all this is going on, Colón also selects key images that he outputs as 4x6-inch prints on a Mitsubishi dye-sublimation printer. At the end of the wedding, he places these in a mini album that the bride and groom can take with them on their honeymoon.

HE PLACES THESE IN A MINI ALBUM THAT THE BRIDE AND GROOM CAN TAKE WITH THEM ON THEIR HONEYMOON.

88. USE METADATA

DSLRs give you the option of tagging your digital image files with data, which typically includes the date, time, a caption, and camera settings for each frame. Many photographers don't even know where to find this information, but it's simple: in Photoshop, go to File>File Info and you will see a range of data. Depending on the camera model, various other information can be written to the file, which can be useful for either the client or lab. You can also add your copyright symbol (©) and notice, either from within Photoshop or from your camera's metadata setup files. Adobe Photoshop supports the information standard developed by the Newspaper Association of America (NAA) and the International Press Telecommunications Council (IPTC) to identify transmitted text and images. This standard includes entries for captions, keywords, categories, credits, and origins from Photoshop.

89. MANAGE COLOR

Why, even in a color-managed system, does the print sometimes look different than the screen image? The answer lies not so much in the color-management process, but in the differences between media. Because monitors and printers have a different color gamut (fixed range of color values), the physical properties of these two different devices make it impossible to show exactly the same colors on your screen and on paper. However, effective color management allows you to align the output from all of your devices to simulate how the color values of your image will be reproduced in a print. This is done using color profiles.

Monitor Profiles. If you set up three identical monitors and had them display the exact same image, they would each look a bit different. This is where profiles come into play. Profiling, which uses a hardware calibration device and accompanying software, characterizes the monitor's output so that it displays a neutral (or at least predictable) range of colors.

A monitor profile is like a color-correction filter. Going back to the example of the three monitors above, one monitor might be slightly green,

OPTIMIZING YOUR WORK AREA

It is recommended that you set your computer desktop to a neutral gray for the purpose of viewing and optimizing images. Because you will most likely make adjustments to color and luminosity, providing a completely neutral, colorless backdrop will help eliminate distractions. Additionally, the room lighting in your work area should also be consistent day to day and throughout the day, and controlled to eliminate any harsh direct lighting on the face of the monitor. This will allow more accurate adjustments to your images and will reduce eyestrain. In general, you should attempt to keep ambient light in the room as low as possible.

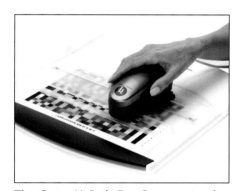

The GretagMcBeth Eye One spectrophotometer comes with a convenient ruler guide and backing board so that the colored wedges of the test print can be read quickly and accurately. The data is then processed to create an ICC profile that gets loaded into the computers that are printing to a specific printer with the profiled paper.

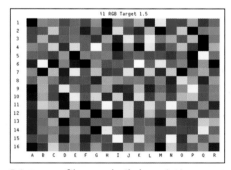

Printer profiles are built by printing a set of known color patches. A spectrophotometer then reads the color patches so the software can interpret the difference between the original file and the printed patches. This is a target that Claude Jodoin uses.

one slightly magenta, and one slightly darker than the other two. Once each monitor is calibrated and profiled, and the resulting profiles are stored in your computer, however, each profile will send a specific correction to the computer's video card, correcting the excess green, magenta, and brightness, respectively, so that all three monitors show the same image identically.

The hardware devices needed for accurate monitor profiling range from relatively inexpensive ($250–$500) to outlandishly expensive (several thousand dollars), but it is an investment you cannot avoid if you are going to get predictable results from your digital systems.

Printer Profiles. Printer profiles are built by printing a set of known color patches from a special digital image file. A spectrophotometer then reads the color patches so the software can interpret the difference between the original file and the actual printed patches. This information is stored in the form of a printer profile, which is then applied to future prints to ensure they are rendered correctly. Custom printer profiles ensure that you are getting the full range of colors that your printer can produce. For best results, use a unique custom profile for each inkjet paper you use.

Custom profiles can be downloaded from the Epson website (www.epson.com) and a variety of other sites. After downloading and printing out the color chart, mail it back to the company, and they will send you a profile or set of profiles via e-mail. Another great source of custom profiles for a wide variety of papers and printers is Dry Creek Photo (www.drycreek photo.com/custom/customprofiles.htm). This company offers a profile-update package so that each time you change ink or ribbons (as in dye-sublimation printing) you can update the profile.

Camera Profiles. DSLRs are used in a wide variety of shooting conditions. This is especially true in wedding photography, where the photographer may encounter a dozen different combinations of lighting in a single afternoon, all with varying intensities and color temperatures. The wedding photographer is looking at a world of color.

Just as all monitors are different, all digital cameras vary at least a little in how they capture color. As a result, some camera manufacturers, like Canon, don't provide device profiles for their cameras.

After all, if the manufacturer made one profile for all their cameras, it would prove somewhat useless. Additionally, there are software controls built into the setup and processing modes for each DSLR that allow photographers sufficient control to alter and correct the color of the captured image.

Creating these custom camera profiles is beneficial if your camera consistently delivers off-color images under a variety of lighting conditions, captures skin tones improperly, or fails to record colors accurately when such precision is critical, such as in the fashion and garment industry. Commercial photographers, for example, often use camera profiles to satisfy the color rendering needs of specific assignments.

90. LEARN PHOTOSHOP, BUT DON'T RELY ON IT

Up until a few years ago, the image was rendered in the camera, but all the magic happened in the darkroom. There are countless great photographers who tell of becoming "hooked" on photography when they first saw a print emerging in the safelight gloom of the developer tray. And who can forget learning to load 35mm film onto stainless-steel reels? It was a badge of courage that made learning the basics of photography seem more rewarding than a post-graduate degree.

PRINTING AND DEVELOPING TECHNIQUES HAVE NOT DISAPPEARED. THEY HAVE BEEN ROLLED INTO PHOTOSHOP . . .

Printing and developing techniques have not disappeared. They have been rolled into Photoshop with tools that far exceed conventional darkroom techniques. Deciding that it provided the most useful language and logic of image enhancement, the designers of Photoshop borrowed heavily from the science of photography. Burning, dodging, cropping, curves, shadow and highlight control, and many other functions are all part of day-to-day operations with Photoshop, just as they are part of the conventional photographic lexicon. Literally everything you could do in the darkroom— except getting brown hypo stains on your clothes and fingernails—can be done in Photoshop, and done better and more extensively.

Still, while Photoshop is an exciting and powerful tool for crafting elegant images, it doesn't pay to become overly reliant on it; great images still begin with great captures. Yervant Zanazanian, an award-winning Australian wedding photographer, puts things in perspective. "A lot of photographers still think it is my tools (digital capture and Photoshop) that make my images what they are. They forget the fact that these are only new tools; imagemaking is in the eye, in the mind, and the heart of a good photographer. During all my talks and presentations, I always remind the audience that you have to be a good photographer first and that you can't

Yervant's great sense of design and flare as an imagemaker have made him one of the most sought-after wedding photographers in the world.

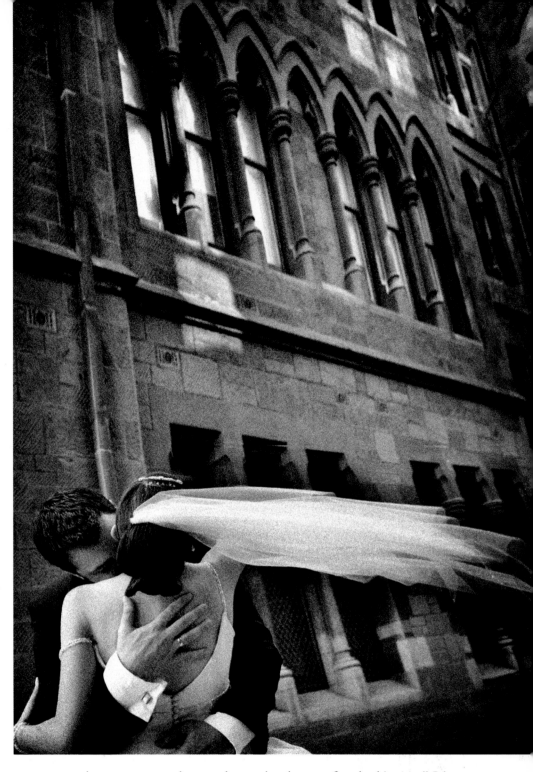

expect, or rely on, some modern tool or technology to fix a bad image." It's good advice.

91. RETOUCH WITH LAYERS
Layers are one of the most flexible tools in Photoshop, because they allow you to work on one element of an image without disturbing the others. Think of layers as sheets of clear acetate stacked one on top of the other;

where there is no image on a layer, you can see through to the layers below. You can change the composition of an image by changing the order and attributes of layers. In addition, special features such as adjustment layers, fill layers, and layer styles let you create sophisticated effects.

When working with layers, get into the habit of naming each layer as you create it. This will help you stay organized. You should also make it your practice to duplicate the background layer before getting started working on an image. This preserves the original, which floats to the bottom of the layers palette. It also opens up creative possibilities, allowing you to alter the new layer and then lower its opacity to allow the original to show through. The eraser tool can also be useful when working on a duplicate of the background layer. For example, you can apply the posterize command (Image>Adjustments>Posterize) to the entire duplicated image layer, then use the eraser tool to reveal the underlying background layer in areas where a more photorealistic look is desired.

TO REMOVE SMALL BLEMISHES, DUST SPOTS, MARKS, OR WRINKLES, SELECT THE HEALING BRUSH TOOL.

92. LEARN TO USE MASKS

Masks are used to temporarily hide portions of a layer. To create a layer mask, activate a layer (other than the background layer) and click on the layer mask icon (the circle in a square) at the bottom of the layers palette. A second thumbnail will appear beside the layer in the layers palette. With black as your foreground color, you can then use the brush tool to paint away (conceal) details in the upper layer, allowing the underlying layer to show through. To reveal the hidden areas again, change the foreground color to white and paint the areas back in. By making changes to the mask, you can apply a variety of special effects to the layer without actually affecting the pixels on that layer. You can then apply the mask and make the changes permanent or remove the mask without applying the changes.

93. REMOVE BLEMISHES

To remove small blemishes, dust spots, marks, or wrinkles, select the healing brush tool. When this tool is selected, an options bar will appear at the top of the screen. Select the normal mode and "sampled" as the source. Choose a soft-edged brush that is slightly larger than the area you are going to repair. Press Opt/Alt and click to sample a nearby area that has the same tone and texture as the area you wish to fix. Then, click on the blemish and the sample will replace it. If the result isn't seamless, hit Command + Z (Edit>Undo), then resample another area and try again. (*Note:* The healing brush differs from the clone tool, another tool commonly used in retouching, in that the healing brush automatically blends the sampled tonality with the area surrounding the blemish or mark.)

94. REDUCE SHININESS AND WRINKLES

These two topics are lumped together because fixing them is easily done using the identical tool and technique. The clone tool, used at an opacity of about 25 percent, is a very forgiving tool that can be applied numerous times in succession to restore a relatively large area. The mode should be set

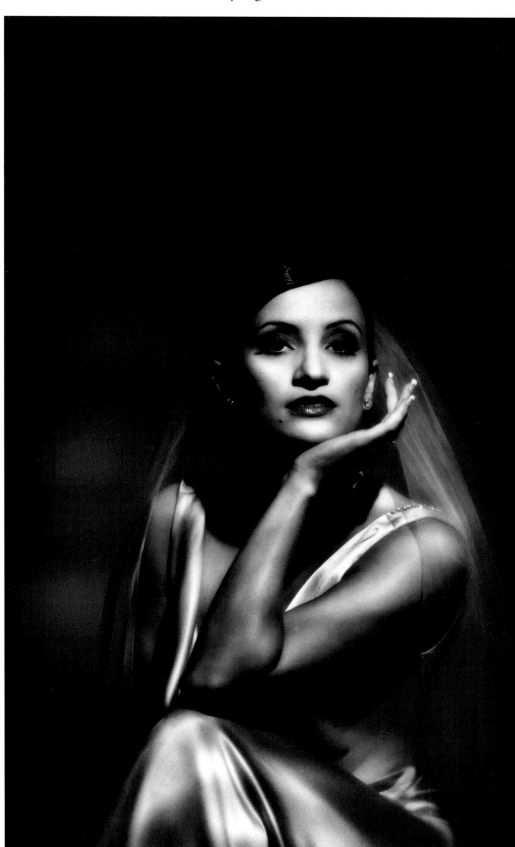

Jerry Ghionis captured this beautiful bride with a Hollywood-style Paramount lighting pattern. He further glamorized the image by adding a soft-focus effect in Photoshop, mimicking the old-fashioned look of on-camera diffusion.

to normal and the brush chosen should be soft-edged. As you would when using the healing brush, sample an area by hitting Opt/Alt and clicking once. A fleeting crosshair symbol shows the sampled area as you apply the tool.

For both wrinkles and areas of shininess, sample an adjacent area with the proper tonality and begin to rework the area. You will find that the more you apply the cloned image data, the lighter the wrinkle becomes or the darker the shiny area becomes. Be sure to zoom out and check to make sure you haven't overdone it. It is important not to remove the highlight or wrinkle entirely, just subdue it. This is one reason why it is always safer to work on a copy of the background layer instead of the original image itself.

95. Add Softening Effects

Selective soft focus is one of the most frequently used retouching effects in wedding and portrait photography. To create this effect, duplicate the background layer and apply the Gaussian blur filter to the new layer. Click the layer mask button to create a mask. With the brush tool selected and the foreground color set to black, start painting away the diffusion from areas like the teeth, eyes, eyebrows, hairline, lips, and bridge of the nose. By varying the opacity and flow you will restore sharpness in the critical areas while leaving the rest of the face pleasingly soft. The best thing is that there will be no telltale sign of your retouching. When you're done, flatten the layers.

SELECTIVE SOFT FOCUS IS ONE OF THE MOST FREQUENTLY USED RETOUCHING EFFECTS IN WEDDING AND PORTRAIT PHOTOGRAPHY.

96. Maximize The Eyes

To make the eyes look their best, create a curves adjustment layer and lighten the overall image by about 20 percent. Click on the layer mask, and go to Edit>Fill>Black to mask the entire layer so that you can see through to the retouched layer underneath. With white as the foreground color, paint over the eyes to lighten them. For a natural and realistic look, you should not make them completely white, nor should you entirely eliminate the natural blood vessels. To increase the color contrast between the pupil and the iris, create a second curves adjustment layer and darken the image slightly. Repeat the rest of the technique as described above, painting over just the pupils to darken them.

Alternately, you can use a small brush and the dodge tool (set to highlights or midtones) to lighten the whites and the interior of the iris. For added drama, use the burn tool and a small brush to trace around just the edge of the iris, darkening it. This increases the edge contrast in the iris for a more dynamic look. You can also burn in the pupil to make it more stark.

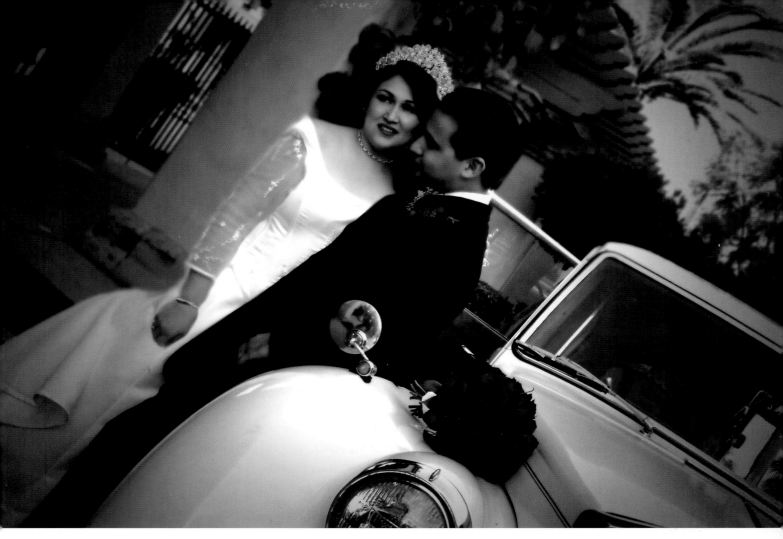

Jerry D, who specializes in digital make-overs, utilized many Photoshop tricks to get this image right. He selectively softened it, vignetted the image with a diffused colored vignette—and then the magic started. The bride asked him to make her slimmer, which he did by removing her arm in Photoshop and pasted it back onto her body, which was made thinner with the liquify filter. You cannot tell where the retouching was done and the bride was ecstatic over Jerry's magic.

97. APPLY THE LIQUIFY FILTER

Liquify is a separate application within Photoshop that lets you push, pull, rotate, reflect, pucker, and bloat any area of an image. The distortions you create can be subtle or drastic, which makes it a powerful tool for retouching images as well as for creating artistic effects. The best way to control your results is to begin by making a selection with the lasso tool. Then go to Filter>Liquify. When your selection comes up, you'll see that it has a brush with a crosshair in it. In the panel to the right, you can adjust this brush size for more precise control. Gently push the area that you want to shrink or stretch, gradually working it until you form a clean line. Hit Enter, and you will return to the original image with the selection still active— but with your modifications in place.

98. APPLY TONING AND SOFT COLOR

Toning. To add a color tone your image (sepia, blue, or any other color), create a copy of your background layer, then go to Image>Adjustments>Desaturate to create a grayscale image. Adjust the levels at this point, if any contrast or tonal adjustment is needed. Then, go to Image>Adjust-

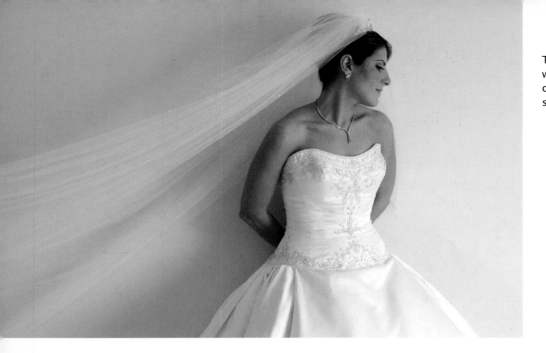

This is a striking mix of sepia and black & white. The image, by Claude Jodoin, was created using the soft-color technique described below.

ments>Selective Color. For a sepia effect, select the neutrals channel and adjust the magenta and yellow sliders. More magenta than yellow will give you a truer sepia tone. More yellow than magenta will give you the look of a brown or selenium image tone. The entire range of warm toners is available using these two controls. For a cool-toned image, either add cyan, reduce yellow, or do both. Again, a full range of cool tones is available in almost infinite variety. (*Note:* Once you have decided on color values you like for these images, you can create actions to automate the process, expediting your image processing.)

Soft Color. This is a technique that mutes the colors in an image. To achieve it, duplicate the background layer and convert it using Image>Adjustments>Gradient Map. Choose a black-to-white gradient for a full-tone black & white image. Then, blur the underlying color layer using the Gaussian blur filter with a radius setting of about 12 pixels. In the layers palette, reduce opacity of the black & white layer to about 65 percent. Add another adjustment layer (Layer>New Adjustment Layer>Photo Filter), then vary the setting of the filter for a range of colored effects.

More yellow than magenta will give you the look of a brown or selenium image tone.

99. Be Smart About Sharpening

Sharpening may have both in-camera and post-production components. In your camera's presets (or in your RAW file processing software) there will be a setting for image sharpening. You should choose the default setting, which is 25 percent. This is the setting recommended by most of the software manufacturers.

The sharpening function in your RAW file processor relates to capture sharpening only, however, and should not be confused with output sharpening for specific devices that is performed in Photoshop. Programs like

Adobe Camera Raw and Lightroom can only perform initial global sharpening; Photoshop is still needed for sharpening specific areas of the image. This selective sharpening (with the Unsharp Mask and/or Smart Sharpen filter) is usually the final step in the image-saving process. (*Note:* To avoid oversharpening in Photoshop, which will product artifacts, go to View>Actual Pixels before performing any sharpening function. This will allow you to best evaluate your results.)

THIS SELECTIVE SHARPENING IS USUALLY THE FINAL STEP IN THE IMAGE-SAVING PROCESS.

Another good tool for sharpening is the Nik Sharpener Pro 2.0 Selective Tool, which allows one to apply any of the program's numerous sharpening filters selectively to your images. Using your mouse or the stylus on your graphics tablet, you can quickly and easily paint sharpening into the image, controlling the amount and location of the sharpening effect.

SINGLE-CHANNEL SHARPENING

If you sharpen the image in the RGB composite channel, you are sharpening all three channels simultaneously. This can lead to color shifts and degradation in quality. Instead, go to the channels palette and look at each channel individually. Sharpen the channel with the most midtones (usually the green channel, but not always), then turn the other two channels back on. This will produce a much finer rendition than sharpening all three channels.

100. USE COLOR SAMPLING

One of Charles Maring's tricks of the trade is sampling colors from the images on his album pages in Photoshop. This is done by using Photoshop's eyedropper tool. When you click on an area, the eyedropper reveals the component colors in either CMYK or RGB in the color palette. He then uses those color readings for graphic elements on the page he designs for those photographs, producing an integrated, color-coordinated design on the album page. If using a page-layout program like QuarkXPress or Adobe InDesign, those colors can be used at 100 percent or any lesser percentage for color washes on the page or background colors that match the Photoshop colors precisely.

CONCLUSION

While the wedding photography industry has flourished in recent years, we are approaching a saturation point and a level of competition between photographers for a dwindling number of high-end weddings. Is there cause for pessimism? I don't think so, because the talented and creative photographer with savvy business and marketing skills will win out every time. There is, however, a need to sharpen and improve your skills, technique, and business acumen if you want to be counted among the photographers who continue to thrive.

Today, a great deal of technology is designed almost specifically for wedding photographers. Ultra-high ISO speeds, simultaneous Wi-Fi transmission of images, radically improved small flash units, and radical new lens designs are all good indicators of a healthy market situation. Camera makers are spending more and more money on research and development, and we are even witnessing the rejuvenation of once-famous brands like Pentax and Olympus. These impressive product offerings for the professional are good signs that the business is here to stay.

The number of new photographers and young photographers is staggering. As trends cycle—in this case, a partial return to more traditional posing and lighting—greater skill and knowledge will be expected of the wedding photographer. I'm constantly amazed at how hard young photographers are working to make up for their lack of experience. Hard work, great ambition, dedication to the craft, and a will to excel are the things that drive these young guns. As the German philosopher Arthur Schopenhauer once said, "Talent hits a target no one else can hit; genius hits a target no one else can see." Gifted wedding photographers, and those who aspire to greatness, are catapulting the art form to new levels of aesthetic and commercial success.

THE TALENTED AND CREATIVE PHOTOGRAPHER WITH SAVVY BUSINESS AND MARKETING SKILLS WILL WIN OUT EVERY TIME.

Nick and Signe Adams. Nick and Signe Adams started Nick Adams Photography in St. George, UT, in 2002. They have been winning awards since they first became WPPI members. They maintain a boutique-type studio business in an historic section of St. George. View their website at www.nickadams.com.

David Beckstead. David Beckstead has lived in a small town in Arizona for twenty-two years. With help from the Internet, forums, digital cameras, seminars, WPPI, Pictage and his artistic background, his passion has grown into a national and international wedding photography business. He refers to his style of wedding photography as "artistic photojournalism."

Marcus Bell. Marcus Bell's creative vision, fluid natural style and sensitivity have made him one of Australia's most revered photographers. It's this talent combined with his natural ability to make people feel at ease in front of the lens that attracts so many of his clients. Marcus' work has been published in numerous magazines in Australia and overseas including *Black White, Capture, Portfolio Bride,* and countless other bridal magazines.

Joe Buissink. Joe Buissink is an internationally recognized wedding photographer from Beverly Hills, CA. Almost every potential bride who picks up a national bridal magazine will have seen Joe Buissink's inspiring photography. He has photographed numerous celebrity weddings, including Christina Aguilera's 2005 wedding, and is a multiple Grand Award winner in WPPI print competition.

Mark Cafeiro. Mark graduated from the University of Northern Colorado with a degree in Business Administration with special emphasis in Marketing. He is the owner of several photography businesses, including Pro Photo Alliance, an online proofing solution for labs and professional photographers, and his own private wedding, event, and portrait business.

Ben Chen. Ben Chen is a freelance photojournalist located in Southern California. He is best known for his award-winning sports photographs, which have been published in the nation's leading magazines and newspapers. Ben has recently become a wedding photographer and is using his instincts as a photojournalist to build his business. Visit his website at: www.socalpixels.com.

Jessica Claire. Jessica Claire graduated from North Carolina State University and has studied with photographers all over the country, from North Carolina to Hawaii.

Mike Colón. Mike Colón is a celebrated wedding photojournalist from the San Diego area. Colón's natural and fun approach frees his subjects to be themselves, revealing their true personality and emotion. His images combine inner beauty, joy, life, and love frozen in time forever. He has spoken before national audiences on the art of wedding photography.

Michael Costa. Michael Costa is an award-winning photographer who graduated with honors from the world-renowned Brooks Institute of Photography in Santa Barbara, CA, receiving the coveted Departmental Award in the Still Photography program. He started his successful business with his wife, Anna during his last year at Brooks.

Cherie Steinberg Coté. Cherie Steinberg Coté began her photography career as a photojournalist at the *Toronto Sun,* where she had the distinction of being the first female freelance photographer. She currently lives in Los Angeles and has recently been published in the *L.A. Times, Los Angeles Magazine,* and *Town & Country.*

Jerry D. Jerry D owns and operates Enchanted Memories, a successful portrait and wedding studio in Upland, CA. Jerry has had several careers in his lifetime, from licensed cosmetologist to black belt martial arts instructor. Jerry is a highly decorated photographer by WPPI and has achieved many national awards since joining the organization.

Jesh de Rox. Canadian photographer Jesh de Rox burst onto the wedding photography scene at the 2006 WPPI convention, where 38 of his entries scored 80 or above. He now teaches all over the country, has a growing wedding business, and is the author and designer of *Fine Art Textures,* available at www.jeshderox.com.

Dan Doke. Daniel has a drive for perfection, abundant creativity, and special eye for light and form. He is a modern photographer with traditional skills, who draws on his experience in commercial, fashion, and portrait photography to create memorable wedding images.

Mauricio Donelli. Mauricio Donelli is a world-famous wedding photographer from Miami, FL. His work is a combination of styles, consisting of traditional photojournalism with a twist of fashion and art. His weddings are photographed in what he calls, "real time." His photographs have been published in *Vogue, Town & Country,* and many national and international magazines. He has photographed weddings around the world.

Bruce Dorn. Bruce Hamilton Dorn of iDC Photography has twenty years of Hollywood filmmaking experience, which shaped his cinematic style of wedding photography. As a member of the Director's Guild of America, Bruce's commercial clients included McDonalds, Sony, Budweiser, and Ford. Bruce, with his artistic partner and wife Maura Dutra, now offers this award-winning expertise to a select group of artistically-inclined wedding clients.

Jerry Ghionis. Jerry Ghionis of XSiGHT Photography and Video is one of Australia's leading photographers. In 1999, he was honored with the AIPP (Australian Institute of Professional Photography) award for best new talent in Victoria. In 2002, he won the AIPP's Victorian Wedding Album of the Year; a year later, he won the Grand Award in WPPI's album competition.

Greg Gibson. Greg is a two-time Pulitzer Prize winner whose assignments have included three Presidential campaigns, daily coverage of the White House, the Gulf War, Super Bowls, and much more. Despite numerous offers to return to journalism, Greg finds shooting weddings the perfect genre to continually test his skills.

Jo Gram and Johannes Van Kan. Johannes and Jo are the principals at New Zealand's Flax Studios, which caters to high-end wedding clients. Johannes has a background in newspaper photography; Jo learned her skills assisting top wedding photographers. In 2005, they teamed up—and they have been winning major awards in both Australia and New Zealand ever since.

Jeff and Kathleen Hawkins. Jeff and Kathleen operate a high-end wedding and portrait photography studio in Orlando, FL, and are the authors of *Professional Marketing & Selling Techniques for Wedding Photographers* (Amherst Media). Jeff has been a professional photographer for over twenty years. Kathleen holds an MBA and is a past president of the Wedding Professionals of Central Florida (WPCF). They can be reached at www.jeff hawkins.com.

Gene Higa. Gene Higa travels the world doing what he loves: photographing weddings. He is one of the most sought-after wedding photographers in the world. Originally from Los Angeles, Gene makes his home in San Francisco, but calls the world his office. He has been commissioned to photograph weddings in Spain, the Philippines, Peru, India, Italy, Greece, Mexico, Hawaii, Jamaica, Thailand and on and on. For more, visit www.genehiga.com.

Elizabeth Homan. Elizabeth Homan owns and operates Artistic Images, where she is assisted by her husband, Trey, and her parents, Penny and Sterling. Elizabeth holds a BA from Texas Christian University and was the decorated as the youngest Master Photographer in Texas in 1998. She holds many awards, including ten Fujifilm Masterpiece Awards.

Tibor Imely. Owned and operated by Tibor Imely, Imely Photography is known as one of the most prestigious studios in the Tampa Bay area. Tibor has won numerous prestigious awards, including the Accolade of Photographic Mastery and Accolade of Outstanding Achievement from WPPI.

Kevin Jairaj. Kevin is a fashion photographer turned wedding and portrait photographer whose creative eye has earned him a stellar reputation in the Dallas/Fort Worth, TX, area. His web site is: www.kjimages.com.

Claude Jodoin. Claude Jodoin is an award-winning photographer from Detroit, Michigan. He has been involved in digital imaging since 1986 and has not used film since 1999. He is an event specialist, as well as shooting numerous weddings and portrait sessions throughout the year. You can e-mail him at claudej1@aol.com.

Jeff Kolodny. Jeff Kolodny began his career as a professional photographer in 1985 after receiving a BA in Film Production from Adelphi University in New York. Jeff recently relocated his business from Los Angeles to South Florida, where his ultimate goal is to produce digital wedding photography that is cutting edge and sets him apart from others in his field.

Kevin Kubota. Kevin Kubota formed Kubota Photo-Design in 1990 as a solution to stifled personal creativity. The studio shoots a mix of wedding, portrait, and commercial photography, and was one of the early pioneers of pure-digital wedding photography. Kubota is well know for training other photographers to make a successful transition from film to digital.

Tamara Lackey. Tamara Lackey owns a lifestyle portrait and wedding photography studio in North Carolina. Her portraits can be seen on the cover of a variety of publications, including *Premier Baby, Carolina Parent,* and *Adoptive Families Magazine.* Her real weddings are featured in *The Knot Magazine, Weddings Unveiled,* and *The Bride's Book.*

Charles and Jennifer Maring. Charles and Jennifer Maring own Maring Photography Inc. in Wallingford, CT. His parents, also photographers, operate Rlab (resolutionlab.com), a digital lab that does all of the work for Maring Photography and other discriminating photographers. Charles Maring was the winner of WPPI's Album of the Year Award in 2001.

Annika Metsla. Photographer Annika Metsla lives in Estonia, a small country in Eastern Europe between Latvia and Russia, bordering the Baltic Sea and Gulf of Finland. An active member of WPPI, Annika operates a thriving photography and wedding planning business, and has recently won a number of awards in WPPI competitions. Visit her at www.annikametsla.com

Tom Muñoz. Tom Muñoz is a fourth-generation photographer whose studio is in Fort Lauderdale, FL. Tom upholds the classic family traditions of posing, lighting, and composition, yet is 100-percent digital. He believes that the traditional techniques blend perfectly with exceptional quality of digital imaging.

Gordon Nash. Gordon Nash owns A Paradise Dream Wedding, one of Hawaii's largest and most successful wedding photography and coordination businesses. He also developed a second, lower-end wedding company called Aekai Beach, staffed by younger photographers whom he mentors. To learn more, visit www.gordonnash.com and www.mauiwedding.net.

Laura Novak. Laura Novak is a studio owner in Delaware. She has achieved more than a dozen Accolades of Excellence from WPPI print competitions. She is also a member of PPA and the Wedding Photojournalist Association of New Jersey. Laura's work can be seen in wedding magazines across the country, including *Modern Bride* and *The Knot*.

Michael O'Neill. As an advertising and editorial photographer who specializes in people, personalities, and product illustration, Michael O'Neill has worked clients including Nikon USA, The New York Jets, Calvin Klein, and Avis. Finding his editorial style of portraiture being the most sought after of his creations, Michael narrowed his specialty to producing portraits—not only for large corporate concerns, but for a discriminating retail market as well.

Joe Photo. Joe Photo's wedding images have been featured in numerous publications such as *Grace Ormonde's Wedding Style*, *Elegant Bride*, *Wedding Dresses*, and *Modern Bride*. His weddings have also been seen on NBC's *Life Moments* and Lifetime's *Weddings of a Lifetime* and *My Best Friend's Wedding*.

Ray Prevost. Ray Prevost worked for 27 years as a medical technologist in the Modesto, CA area. He was always interested in photography but it wasn't until his two daughters were in college that he decided to open up his studio full time. He received Certification from PPA in 1992, and his masters degree in 1996.

JB and DeEtte Sallee. Sallee Photography has only been in business since 2003, but it has already earned many accomplishments. In 2004, JB received the first Hy Sheanin Memorial Scholarship through WPPI. In 2005, JB and DeEtte were also named Dallas Photographer of The Year.

Michael Schuhmann. Michael Schuhmann of Tampa Bay, FL, is an acclaimed wedding photojournalist who believes in creating weddings with the style and flair of the fashion and bridal magazines. He says, "I document weddings as a journalist and an artist, reporting what takes place, capturing the essence of the moment." He has been the subject of profiles in *Rangefinder* magazine and *Studio Photography & Design* magazine.

Kenneth Sklute. Kenneth began his career in Long Island, and now operates a thriving studio in Arizona. He has been named Long Island Wedding Photographer of The Year (fourteen times!), PPA Photographer of the Year, and APPA Wedding Photographer of the Year. He has also earned numerous Fuji Masterpiece Awards and Kodak Gallery Awards.

Steve Tarling. After having freelanced in travel, fashion, wedding, and industrial photography since leaving art school in 1985, Steve Tarling established A Little Box of Memories. He is now an in-demand speaker on contemporary wedding photography. Steve was also named Great Britain's 2003 Wedding Photographer of the Year.

Marc Weisberg. Marc Weisberg specializes in wedding and event photography. A graduate of UC Irvine with a degree in fine art and photography, he also attended the School of Visual Arts in New York City before relocating to Southern California in 1991. His images have been featured in *Wines and Spirits*, *Riviera*, *Orange Coast Magazine*, and *Where Los Angeles*.

David Anthony Williams (*M.Photog. FRPS*). Williams operates a wedding studio in Ashburton, Victoria, Australia. In 1992, he was awarded Associateship and Fellowship of the Royal Photographic Society of Great Britain (FRPS). In 2000, he was awarded the Accolade of Outstanding Photographic Achievement from WPPI. He was also a Grand Award winner at their annual conventions in both 1997 and 2000.

Jeffrey and Julia Woods. Jeffrey and Julia Woods are award-winning wedding and portrait photographers who work as a team. They were awarded WPPI's Best Wedding Album of the Year for 2002 and 2003, two Fuji Masterpiece awards, and a Kodak Gallery Award. See more of their images at www.jwweddinglife.com.

Yervant Zanazanian (*M. Photog. AIPP, F.AIPP*). Yervant was born in Ethiopia (East Africa), where he worked after school at his father's photography business (his father was photographer to the Emperor Hailé Silassé of Ethiopia). Yervant owns one of the most prestigious photography studios of Australia and services clients both nationally and internationally.

Regina and Denis Zaslavets. Denis and Regina are originally from Odessa, Ukraine. She has resided in the U.S. for 27 years and Denis only three years. They own Assolux Photography, a small studio where they do portraiture for adults and children, formal engagements, and family portraits—but weddings, which they cover as a team, are their main passion.

INDEX

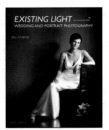
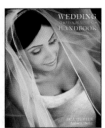
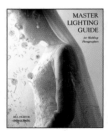
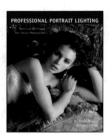
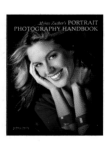
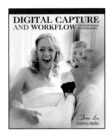
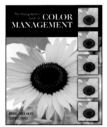